Tommy Hinnershitz

The
Life and
Times of an
Auto-
Racing
Legend

TOMMY HINNERSHITZ
The Life and Times of an
Auto-Racing Legend

by Gary Ludwig

Copyright © 2009 by Gary Ludwig

Library of Congress Control Number: 2009900178

ISBN 10: Hardcover 0-9815099-4-0

ISBN 13: Hardcover 978-0-9815099-4-5

This book was manufactured in the United States of America.

Basket Road Press, Inc.
Harrisburg, PA USA

Second Edition - 2010

To order additional books contact:
info@basketroadpress.com

WWW.BASKETROADPRESS.COM

To Beth;
You're always on my mind.

To Christine, Daniel and Elijah

In memory of Marcia and John,
Mom and Dad

In memory of Uncle Floyd Delp, a tough cigar smoking trucking executive who was always kind to me. When I was a kid, he let me tag along. Just before he died, he encouraged me to write a book about Tommy Hinnershitz.

In memory of race historian Carl Sweigart, who spent many hours teaching me about auto-racing. His historical compilations, along with official records, have made it possible to include Tommy Hinnershitz's career statistics in this book.

Acknowledgments

To editor Cassandra Kane: all authors need a good editor. Cassandra used her accomplished editing skills to refine the manuscript and help make it a book.

To Joanne Thomas: her efficient composition know-how and excellent interior design talents resulted in an attractive, readable book.

To Beth Ludwig: my wife and assistant. Her administrative, logistical, and research services have always been invaluable to my work. She made sure the project went forward.

Special thanks to Tommy Hinnershitz's daughters Jeanne Hinnershitz Craig and Carol Hinnershitz Bruckart for the cooperation, support, and encouragement they provided while I wrote this book.

I want to particularly thank the following people who, among others, gave their time and provided me with valuable insight, documents, or photographs essential to writing a factual account of the *early years* of automobile racing.

Marty Himes, Racing Historian
Dan Holynski
Barbara Holynski
Ernie (McCoy) Musser, Jr.
Bill Nash, Racing Historian
Vicki Nunis
Lynn Paxton
Steve Pryor, Oswego Speedway
Ellen Riegel
Joe Ruffilo, Paterson Museum
Gordon White, Racing Historian
Joy Whitfield, Will Rogers Coliseum

Paul J. Boltz, President, Pennsylvania Sports Hall of Fame
Ralph Hibbard Jr., Greenfield Gallery
Paul Menhenett, President, Miracle Power Products Corporation

We proudly sponsored the *Miracle Power Special* Sprint car driven by legendary racecar driver

Tommy Hinnershitz

Miracle Power
Products Corporation

Cleveland, Ohio

HS-HL Engine Lubricant
Concentrated Oil Supplement
Dry Graphite Film
Wet Graphite Film
Engine Lubricant

We applaud the publishing of this book that celebrates Tommy's career and affords people the opportunity to read about his phenomenal accomplishments during a career that spanned five decades.

About the Author

Gary Ludwig began his career in radio, working as a producer, copywriter, news and sports writer, marketing manager, morning radio host, and country music on-air disc jockey.

He began working in advertising, and before that was a columnist for the weekly auto-racing tabloid *Illustrated Speedway News* and at the same time wrote and anchored news segments on the *Speedsport Commentary Radio Network.*

Later he founded a regional magazine in Central Pennsylvania writing commentary and feature articles while serving as publisher.

He wrote a series of magazine articles about a 19th-century Pennsylvania murder and is interviewed in the Kreider Brothers documentary film about the crime.

Ludwig's gritty crime and romance novel *Mexico Road* was published in 2006, followed by fantasy novel *The Angels and Demons of Hamlin* in 2008.

He continues to reside in Pennsylvania and works as a writer of fiction and non-fiction.

Cover Photographs

Front Dust Jacket Photograph

Tommy Hinnershitz poses in the cockpit of the Miracle Power Special in 1955. Photograph is compliments of the Reading, Pennsylvania Fairgrounds.

Back Dust Jacket Photograph

Tommy Hinnershitz poses in the Miracle Power Special at the Reading, Pennsylvania Fairgrounds circa 1953. Photograph is compliments of Miracle Power Products Corporation.

Table of Contents

Tommy Hinnershitz poses in the cockpit of the Miracle Power Special in 1955.

Preface

In 1928 Tommy Hinnershitz began his career as a racecar driver. He became one of the greatest athletes in all of sports. He became an automobile racing legend. Hinnershitz was there at the beginning, one of a handful of daredevil athletes—the *champions*, who invented the broad slide, going in low and coming off high, or vice versa. After leading the way, setting the pace, and developing the style, he set himself apart from all the others; he went in high and stayed there. In the days before night racing and cool, moist clay surfaces, broad sliding in the turns up against the outside fence was difficult because the racetrack—watered down before the racing began—would dry out, break up, and turn to dust as the competition went on under the blazing hot summer sun. He mastered the art of running high in the turns despite those adverse track conditions. While his competitors were racing close to the inside rail, he powered his car around them. Racing Sprint cars on dirt in the *modern years* (after 1960) under the lights on clay surfaces and using much wider tires enables virtually every driver to race the way only Hinnershitz did.

He was a true pioneer of American dirt track automobile racing, competing during the *early years* in racecars without seat belts, roll bars, cages, fire extinguishers, and other modern safety equipment. Hinnershitz feared most the thought of being burned seriously or burned to death. He was forced to ignore the absence of safety equipment and corresponding safety rules. He and his contemporaries, during the *early years*, seemed to embrace a greater lack of fear, adopting the adage that tragedy can't or won't happen to them, only to the "other guy."

Because Midgets, smaller cars built to run mostly on third-mile or quarter-mile racetracks, became very popular during the 1930s, Sprint cars were called "Big cars" until about 1950. They were bigger in size with bigger motors and more horsepower to race on larger, primarily half-mile tracks. The modern name Sprint car is used throughout this book, even when referring to them during the *early years*.

The *early years* was the era when auto-racing was founded, punctuated by numerous deaths and serious injury to drivers each racing season. The sport stole the lives of so many—in the aftermath filling the sleeping tracks and darkened infields with ghosts while leaving only faint memories of the fallen greats.

Because of innovative engineering, ingenuity, and hard labor, powerful and dependable engines came of age. The brave *champions* of the *early years* tortured those engines, forcing them to scream and whine—extorting yet more and more speed or blowing them to pieces. Despite all the peril, American ambition and determination required that it be done. The *champions* lived, and some died, doing what they loved most.

As in other sports at the championship level, *modern day* competitors have learned much from pioneers and innovators. Lessons taught by Hinnershitz in word and deed are the most treasured, and his legacy will live on because he was an analytical and highly focused racecar driver with an original, artistic style of driving.

He was a kind man who made everyone he met feel important. He would smile at you, shake your hand, and be your friend. But his contemporaries, and also the drivers of the *modern years* who pay attention, realized he was a fierce predator on the racetrack, determined to chase down and beat anybody who tried to outrun him.

He explained how he did it, that it took him a few laps to get into position to pass a man, then he'd wait for the right moment to complete the pass, the same way a lion stalks its prey. He emphasized that skill and thoroughness are the essential ingredients. He steered mostly with his foot, describing how lifting the throttle slows the car going into the turns and gets the car sideways. Feeding the throttle just right while going through the turn kept the car in the power slide and enabled him to get into position to jump down the straightaway. He used the steering wheel to keep the car steady. Hinnershitz was the master, if not the inventor of the controlled power slide. Rumors that he intentionally slowed his time trials to place him on an outside row starting position had persisted for years. But that was just talk. He stressed that a good qualifying run is the most important challenge in a Sprint car race; heat race starts are inverted, meaning the fast cars start in the back, while in the feature, it's fast man up front. Setting good time and starting up front saves a lot of wear and tear on the car by not having to do so much passing.

In his 32 years as a national championship racecar driver, Hinnershitz was Eastern AAA (American Automobile Association) Sprint Car Champion five times, Eastern USAC (United States Auto Club) Sprint Car Champion two times, and runner-up for the AAA title six times. His career resume includes 103 victories, 93 second-place finishes, and 57 third-place finishes. He was the holder of 32 track records at time of retirement. He scored more points in Sprint car competition, both AAA and USAC, than any other driver in the history of the sport. His 103 victories is the all-time record for feature wins in AAA and USAC Sprint car competition. His wins and other top placing finishes came during an era when Sprint cars typically competed in just one race per week, mostly on state and county fair horse tracks throughout the country.

He raced in the Indianapolis 500 three times, finishing 32nd in 1940, 10th in 1941, and 9th in 1948.

Hinnershitz received many honors during his long career and afterward during retirement, including his induction into the Pennsylvania Sports Hall of Fame, the National Sprint Car Hall of Fame, the Motorsports Hall of Fame of America, and the Eastern Museum of Motor Racing Hall of Fame.

The Family at the Races

Daughters Jeanne and Carol knew not to bother their mother when the racing was going on. They would each go their separate ways.

Betty Hinnershitz needed to be by herself; that was her way of dealing with the deafening whining of the Offenhauser engines, the torrid high-speed broad sliding and furious maneuvering through the blinding thick clouds of dust as the *champions* frantically raced into the turns, drawn dangerously close together, friendships temporarily lost to competition as they sought to outmatch one another during their unyielding push to lead the pack.

It was serious business. She watched for any racecars getting airborne. She knew if that happened, tragedy could descend upon her like a heavy, crushing black cloud.

If their father was in an accident, the girls were told not to go near it.

And they were not to come to her.

Betty would be going to him.

Introduction

Starting when I was a 14 year-old kid, I would go to the Sunday afternoon Sprint car races at the famous half-mile dirt track at the Reading Fairgrounds in Pennsylvania, about two or three miles from my house. I usually went alone because none of my friends had any money. In those days, the Sprint cars only raced two, sometimes three times a year in Reading. On one of those Sundays, I encountered Jud Larson, covered with mud and sweat, carrying his trophies. He noticed my racing program in one hand, my pen in the other, and the look of disappointment on my face. Without being asked, he put all the trophies down on the ground and autographed his photo. I still have it.

I waited all winter to see the famous *champions* and the shiny, beautifully painted and chromed racing machines, most owned by men of means and driven by men who were chasing that well-known dream of competing in the Indianapolis 500. Others had already been there, some with success, others sent packing.

Starting a couple of weeks before the races, the local sports page each day featured photos and biographies of the drivers who informed the local fair board of their intention to compete. This publicity created a great deal of excitement among the race fans anticipating to see, in person, the famous racecar drivers they heard on the radio competing at Indianapolis. Everyday I rushed home from school to read the paper and learn about the latest entry. Of course, the biggest write-up appeared in the Sunday morning edition on race day. Featured in that story, along with a large photograph, was the most famous Sprint car driver ever, the local hero, the farmer from Oley, Pennsylvania—Tommy Hinnershitz.

I never seemed to get there early enough. I'd get my dad to give me a ride to the track, passing the Bellevue Diner on the way hoping to see pick-up trucks with out-of-state license plates pulling their trailers hauling the beautiful racecars glistening in the morning sun. I hoped A.J. Foyt would be there eating breakfast, or maybe Parnelli Jones, or Jim Hurtibuise and Bobby Unser, all of them arriving in town just an hour or two earlier. But they had their coffee and had already driven a mile down the Fifth Street highway to the fairgrounds.

While I eagerly waited in line for my ticket, I listened to the announcer's blaring voice and earsplitting echoes on the loudspeaker thanking everyone and promoting everything imaginable. I listened to the hawkers howling while walking up and down the steps in the grandstand aisles selling hot dogs, hamburgers, French fries, cold drinks, coffee or hot chocolate, and racing programs. One peddler in particular had a shrilled voice with the intensity of an air raid siren: "coooooold drinks," he shouted. The line leading to the ticket window never moved quickly enough, and the ultimate frustration was hearing the cars being pushed off, the Offenhauser engines firing up, as the warm-up part of the program began before I could get to my seat.

I'd stand along the fence just as the fourth turn entered the front straightaway so I could be just a few feet from my hero, Tommy Hinnershitz, as he rumbled by warming up the racecar's engine. His face shield was up; only his goggles partially obscured his facial features. On this day he was driving the John Pfrommer-owned car, a beautiful powder blue and white Sprint car. Something new was evident; Hinnershitz was wearing red gloves instead of the basic brown work ones he usually wore to drive. Later I learned from general store owner Bill Delp that when Hinnershitz came in earlier in the week for a pair of brown gloves, only red ones were in stock. Farmers usually don't buy red work gloves, but a farmer that also drives racecars evidently did. They were pleasant to the eyes of the 10,000 or so race fans, a great contrast to the car's blue and white colors and Hinnershitz's blue coveralls that he used as a driver's suit.

When I saw him nodding his head I quickly looked up at the starter holding his flags on the high tower and acknowledging the signal, while he held the yellow flag draped over the railing, flapping in the breeze. This went on for a few laps. Finally Hinnershitz raised his arm and held up his finger giving the one more lap sign. It was a crowd pleaser to give Hinnershitz the green flag for hot laps first. I experienced up close the breathtaking experience of witnessing him, all in one swift move, flip down his face shield with his right hand while his left turned the steering wheel to the right as the rear end and all hell broke loose as a result of his foot pounding the throttle to the cockpit's floor. I watched as he roared down the straightaway and threw the car sideways into the first turn. I turned and looked up at the grandstand crowd—all were standing and cheering.

About half of the 150 or so kids' classrooms at Alsace Township Consolidated School had windows that faced the two-lane blacktop Antietam Road. On some Monday mornings in spring or early fall, the lucky kids who weren't paying attention to their schoolwork got to see the blue Dodge pick-up truck passing by the school pulling a trailer carrying the most beautiful blue and yellow Sprint car in the world, with that big red number on its tail. Many kids knew he had been far away racing, maybe in Illinois, Indiana or Wisconsin, but on a Monday morning, where he'd been didn't matter; it was only important that he returned home safe. During those *early years*, some drivers never came home. The great "Miracle Power Special" was put away, and for the next few days, Hinnershitz would work the fields and the garage.

In my teen years, my Uncle Floyd Delp would occasionally phone on a Sunday morning: "If you want to go along, get over here. I'm leaving shortly." I didn't know what he meant when he said "shortly," but I knew if I wasn't there on time he'd leave without me. I peddled my bicycle to his house as fast as I could, hoping not to miss the ride. It was a great experience for a kid, traveling with men who were professionals in the sport of auto-racing. I wanted to learn, so I listened to every word they spoke. There was German immigrant George Keorner, a retired master mechanic and car builder who fled to America when Hitler came to power. Upcoming driver Red Riegel tagged along hoping to get a ride when we got to whatever track we were headed for that day. Future noted auto-racing photographer Bruce Craig, who later married Tommy and Betty Hinnershitz's daughter Jeanne, joined us every now and then. There were others who jumped aboard from time to time. Sometimes Hinnershitz's brothers Cal and Bobby would go along—the Delp and Hinnershitz clans were related. It seemed like everyone in Alsace Township during those years were related, many of the family farms were connected.

Uncle Floyd learned everything he knew about racecars from Hinnershitz. Back in the 1950s, Floyd built two stock cars, the kind that eventually evolved to become modified stock cars, and later built and owned Sprint cars. He and Riegel were in the trucking business together at the same time that Red was pursuing a career as a racecar driver.

For me the sights, sounds, and smells of state and county fairs have always been intoxicating. To this day, I love to experience the barking carnies, fortune tellers, girlie show dancers, strong men and weight guessers, the loud music from the amusement rides and grandstand shows, and the smell of French fries, hot dogs, hamburgers and sausage sandwiches with fried onions. I was drawn so much to it all that I left home and traveled the fair circuit, just days after graduating from high school, to try and satisfy my yearning for the life as a carnie.

Automobile racing is part of that life. Dirt track auto-racing was developed to entertain the fairgoer. I got to meet a lot of different people I'll never forget, from balloon sellers to movie stars, people who were famous, some very famous, but most not famous at all.

My exposure to automobile racing early in my life taught me a lot about the inner workings of the sport, knowledge that prepared me to write and broadcast the news about it. Over the years, whenever I got to talk with Hinnershitz, whether to interview him or just have friendly conversation, I was always able to learn more about auto-racing's past and present.

Listening to him talk about the years when he competed and about the men he raced against was spellbinding.

Uncle Floyd's good friend Carl Sweigart, noted racing historian, former writer, and track announcer, taught me how to cover an auto race. He began teaching me the history of auto-racing in the 1970s while we sat in the press box every Friday night at Williams Grove Speedway in Mechanicsburg, Pennsylvania, and when we brown-bagged lunch at his Harrisburg, Pennsylvania, office during the workweek. Carl was a walking auto-racing encyclopedia, truly one of the greatest auto-racing historians ever. I owe him so very much.

When I was a young reporter, I was no different than many others who preceded me and have followed. I overlooked people, places, and things that were right under my nose. I failed to interview many "old timers" who are no longer here. One of my biggest regrets is not interviewing Ernie McCoy. While covering ARDC Midget events, Ernie and I would exchange hellos. Now, years later, when I look at Ernie's career statistics, at his accomplishments, I realize how much he was overlooked and underrated. It is my loss that I didn't have the foresight to sit with him for an extended interview.

American automobile racing had its beginnings with cars built to race on road courses such as Fairmount Park in Philadelphia and eventually at the Indianapolis Motor Speedway. Later the cars evolved into what the AAA Contest Board called "Championship cars." This division of cars raced on dirt and pavement, primarily on one-mile tracks. Later roadsters, Championship cars built low to the ground, were designed specifically to run on pavement, especially at Indianapolis. The original Championship cars, higher off the ground and now labeled "Uprights" or "Dirt Cars," were run only on the dirt tracks, although occasionally some owners would put them on pavement despite the fact they were not competitive running against the roadsters. These "Uprights" became the ancestors of the present day USAC Silver Crown Series division. Sprint cars, originally called "Big cars," were built to race mostly on half-mile paved and dirt tracks, and Midgets were created to compete on third or quarter-mile tracks.

When I'd stop by during the week to see Jack Gunn, promoter at Williams Grove during the 1970s, I'd overhear him tell his secretary, "I can see him but tell him I only have a few minutes." While I asked him the questions I needed answers for, I'd gaze out the large picture window overlooking the first and second turn of the sleeping speedway. When I got the opportunity, I'd sneak into the conversation some obscure bit of racing history. That would prompt Jack to talk about the *early years*, talking much longer than I expected about Tommy Hinnershitz, Ted Horn, Mark Light, Joie Chitwood, and other stars of the past. The main reason for my visit had been to get some current news for the radio network and racing paper I worked for. But I was also searching for still more information about the *early years* to use someday in a book.

On my way out, I asked Jack's secretary to remind him it wasn't my fault that my visit lasted more than an hour. Jack understood a great deal more about newsgathering than most promoters because he was a member of the media before taking over the reins at Williams Grove. Jack died young; his untimely death was a great loss to automobile racing.

I was the guest of many promoters who allowed me full access to the pits. Lindy Vicari, longtime promoter at Reading, and Gunn were especially accommodating. They both produced great auto-racing programs for the fans. I was up in the tower at Reading one night while the racecars were parading around the track under yellow just prior to warm-ups. Lindy came up the stairs and asked the light man if he was going to run the cars under yellow all night. Before Lindy had the question completely out of his mouth, this fellow flipped the green light. The starter, caught by surprise, quickly started waving the green flag as the racecars came flying off the fourth turn. Many times, all Lindy needed to do was ask a question. He spent his life doing hard physical labor in the mushroom growing business. When he got into promoting at Reading, he personally ran the grader while the finishing touches were put on the track surface before race time. Most people aren't aware he developed a brain tumor that affected his speech and thankfully had successful surgery to have it removed.

In 1974, Paul Boltz, president of the Pennsylvania Sports Hall of Fame, asked for my help to get auto-racing *champions* of the past inducted into the hall of fame. I agreed to assist in the effort and considered it an honor to participate. Boltz appointed me to the Central Chapter's Induction Screening Committee. It was a tense assignment for me. I knew if I couldn't get Hinnershitz nominated, I would take the loss badly and feel personally responsible. There were men on the committee who knew nothing about auto-racing. Hinnershitz was nominated that night at the Timbers Restaurant in Mt. Gretna, Pennsylvania. I was also successful in getting India-napolis 500 relief driver and Lebanon, Pennsylvania, native Cyrus Patschke nominated.

Hinnershitz and Patschke got on the ballot and both were elected to the Central Chapter Hall of Fame by chapter members. The following year, Hinnershitz was inducted into the Pennsylvania Sports Hall of Fame after being chosen overwhelmingly by members from all over the state.

When I was preparing the press release announcing Hinnershitz's induction, I went into the Reading Fairgrounds office after the races one night and asked Lindy if he could loan me a photograph of Hinnershitz from the Reading Fair publicity files. Without saying a word, he turned, reached up, and took down the large framed photograph of Hinnershitz that hung on the wall in the fairground's office for years. He handed it to me and without waiting for me to recover, he walked into his office while I made sure he heard my thank you and my assurance the photo will be returned. The media members and officials who were crowded in the room were dazed; looks of disbelief were showing on most of their faces.

Most of us are blessed with fond memories and our ability to recall and rejoice about the highpoints of our lives and also to deal with the mistakes everyone makes. During our lives, we all acquire heroes. Hinnershitz became a hero to thousands of people all over America. His achievements as an athlete are overwhelming. We use people like him as a model when we mold our lives and establish our own standards. If each of us works hard and develops the discipline necessary to reach our goals, we can enjoy our own versions of success.

This book is about the life and times of Tommy Hinnershitz. Inevitably, memories in the minds and hearts of the people who lived those times with him fade and then die. This book allows some of those people no longer here the opportunity to share their memories.

Chapter 1

The Beginning

Thomas Paul "Tommy" Hinnershitz became one of the legends of American automobile racing, and when invention and innovation are taken into account, he was the greatest Sprint car driver that ever lived. He was a true *champion*, a pioneer of the sport during *the early years* who, during the twilight years of his phenomenal career also left his mark in the record books of the *modern days*.

An English translation of the German name Hinnershitz is *rear guard*. The family began in America with Johann George, who spelled his last name "Hinterschied." Later, some family members spelled their name Hinnerschietz and Hinnerschitz, and eventually many adopted the spelling Hinnershitz. Johann George was born in April, 1724, in Germany. Sketchy records of those times have him and his wife Maria Catherine traveling to Holland and then sailing from Rotterdam on their journey while Maria Catherine was carrying their first child. Passenger logs show them landing in the Port of Philadelphia on the ship Edinburgh on September 15, 1749. After staying in Philadelphia for a short while, they moved to Alsace Township, Berks County, Pennsylvania, where they first appeared on the tax list in 1768. Johann and Maria were among early German settlers who came to American to live the dream of escaping serfdom and to farm their own land. Their strong work ethic continues to be passed down to new generations.

Both Johann and Maria are buried in Spies's Church Cemetery in Alsace Township and are said to be two of the founders of the Lutheran church there. This same cemetery is also the final resting place of Tommy and Betty Hinnershitz.

Most Pennsylvania German people of Hinnershitz's generation, and certainly those of his parents, spoke the Pennsylvania Dutch dialect much of the time. In fact, as late as 1950, first-grade students were showing up at Alsace Consolidated School who could only speak Pennsylvania Dutch. The dialect is ultimately a derivative of the Palatinate German language. The origin of "Dutch" is a corruption or a "folk-rendering" of the term "Deitsch," mostly by the English colonist's mispronunciation. The English word for Deitsch is "German." Also, many thought these Germans were in fact Dutch because their voyage began in Rotterdam.

The area of Pennsylvania consisting of Berks County and neighboring counties is unique, the people a product of a convergence of many cultures and many dialects. The German immigrants became neither English nor German but something in between. Their English language speech remained influenced by the German language, sustained mostly because of the continued use of the dialect. But by the 1960s, most of the young people of the post-World War II generation abandoned the dialect, speaking only English, but it was and continues to this day to be heavily accented "Dutchified English." Many strangers quickly notice Pennsylvania Germans' accent when they travel out of the area.

Hinnershitz was born to Allen "Al" or "Allie" and Florence "Floss" (Feeg) Hinnershitz in Berks County on April 6, 1912. At the time of Hinnershitz's birth, farming was the way of life in this beautiful and peaceful part of Pennsylvania. Hinnershitz learned early to do farm work, laboring on his father's farm in nearby Muhlenberg Township. He attended his first auto race around 1925 at the Reading Fairgrounds, only about a mile or two from the Hinnershitz farm. The eight-year-old, like his friends, didn't have any money, so they jumped the fence or crawled under it. He went back again and again.

In 1928 famed *champion* Billy Arnold became Hinnershitz's hero, his first idol, when he saw him fearlessly circle the Reading track. At that early age, Hinnershitz already decided he wanted to be a racecar driver, and the 16-year-old soon got his chance to race on the half-mile that he would always consider his home track. He entered the 1928 competition when Berks County residents were given the opportunity to race Model Ts. In this first race, he led for a while but faded because his car kept getting slower while the others got faster. An overdose of ether added to the fuel evidently caused the problem. Hinnershitz bought three jars at the drugstore and added one to energize the motor. Two of his buddies, acting as his pit crew, didn't know Hinnershitz already added a jar, so they each added a jar. The overdose thwarted Hinnershitz's efforts that day.

In 1931 he bought a 1914 Model T for $25 and raced it to victory, winning $75 in prize money. He now realized that he needed to get real serious building a racecar and learning how to drive it. His Dodge powered car was built with junk parts, and according to Hinnershitz, it was an awkward looking thing. While kick starting his career as a racecar driver, building this first racecar was the beginning of him mastering the mechanics needed to maintain race engines. Eventually on his farm he set up a machine shop that enabled him to completely disassemble engines, rebuild them, and maintain them in superior running order, doing much of his own tooling and machine work. These developed skills gave him, as a driver, an edge over the competition. He could hear and feel the engine reacting when it was running to perfection, and when it was performing negatively, he could diagnose the trouble and take it home and do whatever was necessary to correct the problem.

At that point he knew very little about driving fast, but he learned by trial and error, bending the car up numerous times. Pretty soon it was so banged up it was worthless, and he eventually took it back to the junkyard. More importantly, even though the car was damaged beyond redemption, Hinnershitz wasn't. Luckily he escaped injury. But it wasn't all because of luck. Farm work kept him in top physical condition that resulted in great strength in his legs and arms along with superior stamina. He could man-handle the racecar, and each lap on the dirt track was just one more lesson in high speed racecar driving. He learned how deep he could go into the turns before backing off. He watched the other drivers, eyeing up their weaknesses and strong points. He knew all he had to do to beat them was be the driver with the fastest car.

In 1932 he entered his first AAA event, the Spring opener at Reading. While Fred Frame was satisfying the paying customers, Hinnershitz was having problems. He entered his own car, a four cylinder Dodge, went six laps, and then took down a few sections of fence.

He started the 1933 season in his own Model T. He had a hard time keeping the car running long enough to finish the race. Later in the season he ran a rocker-arm Model T Fronty owned by Sandy Novak and Paul Kolson of Allentown, Pennsylvania

His physical strength—he was a muscular 5'7" and weighed 182 pounds—was matched by the mental strength of a stubborn "Pennsylvania Dutchman." He was determined to be successful. Like any athlete, to become a *champion* you have to make a strong commitment. You have to stay at it and brush aside the failures as well as savor the successes. Hinnershitz started to discover some success after building a better car.

What was possibly the greatest factor in his long successful career was his ability to take advantage of good or bad situations in which he found himself. He had the awesome ability to completely focus and aggressively compete against all comers, all those other guys who were hell-bent for glory. He was determined to overcome all resistance and go on to win if at all possible. He discovered the ingredients to be a *champion*.

He developed habits early on to increase his odds for victory. From the time the racecar was loaded on the trailer until he was pushed off for warm-ups, he remained calm and kept busy preparing the car and himself for racing. When he arrived at a racetrack, no matter if he raced there before or if it was the first time, he walked around the entire length of the track, observing among other things the track's condition, parts to avoid if possible, and the parts to run on while searching for the groove. He checked the banking and depth of the turns, the length of the straight-aways, and any unique characteristics. During those *early years*, before clay was used on track surfaces, track conditions could change quickly during the course of a racing program and often did.

About 10 or 15 years earlier, auto races were run on road courses using public streets. After several instances when racecars veered off the course and killed and maimed spectators, most American auto-racing had moved from the public streets to the horse tracks of the state and county fairs. In 1900, Point Breeze Racetrack, which now lies under the Philadelphia Airport, became the first Pennsylvania horse racetrack to host auto-racing and is considered by many to be the birthplace of American automobile racing. Unfortunately, Point Breeze also became the site of the first racecar driver killed in Pennsylvania. Ernest Keeler flipped his racecar during practice on November 23, 1906. Two years later, organized auto-racing began on a road course in Philadelphia's Fairmount Park. On the horse tracks, racing became less technically interesting and more a form of entertainment. Speeding racecars driven by daredevil heroes had become ever increasingly popular and profitable. The next step in the evolution of the sport occurred in 1926. That year the directors of the National Motor Racing Association decided to build America's first racetrack specifically to race automobiles. They built a one-mile dirt track in Langhorne, Pennsylvania, an area on the outskirts of Philadelphia. They built it almost perfectly round so it would fit on their 89 acres of swampland.

For the competitors, there was always one big problem while racing on these dirt ovals; they dried out and turned to dust. There were two cures; constantly watering it or putting down a coating of oil that soon mixed with the dirt. This hardened the surface and kept down the dust, but purists didn't acknowledge the resulting surface as a dirt track. Most dirt tracks today are clay, whether indigenous or trucked in from the bottom of some pond or lake. When properly watered and otherwise maintained, a track with a clay surface changes much less during competition and can be safe and fast with little or no dust hanging in the air.

Hinnershitz used the inspections to base decisions on which tires to use, what gearing would be best, how to set-up weight distribution on the racecar, and to try to predict what changes would need to be made to the car as the track changed during the afternoon of racing. It was the type of preparation that was necessary during the *early years*, preparation that only the best professionals bothered to practice. It's what increased Hinnershitz's chances of winning and becoming a *champion*.

In 1934 he stayed on the throttle too long on the backstretch at Reading and landed in the horse barns just outside the third-turn fence. He got out of the car fast thinking others were going to follow. They didn't. Despite this unfortunate misjudgment, he had matured into a good enough racecar driver to get the attention of some car owners, and they began to consider giving him a ride. Parke Culp and his brother George "Dutch" Culp were running a racing team out of Allentown. They decided to give the young upstart a chance. Hinnershitz joined the team as the third driver. Later tragedy struck on September 7, 1936, when Parke was killed in one of the Culp Sprint cars at Flemington, New Jersey. He was wearing a helmet he borrowed from Hinnershitz. Future Indianapolis 500 star Eddie Sachs, who was also from Allentown, got a big part of his racing education when he tagged along with Dutch Culp and his crew. Hinnershitz's driving talents kept improving steadily, fueled by more and more experience, intuition, and natural instincts.

On November 23, 1935, Hinnershitz married the former Betty Selman of Lebanon, Pennsylvania. She met him through her friend June Plantz, who had been dating Lebanon racecar driver Mark Light. June and Light eventually got married. Light reopened the Lebanon Fairgrounds that previous spring, introducing Sprint car racing to Central Pennsylvania. Hinnershitz was earning about $1 a week working for his father when he married Betty. Struggling financially, the newlyweds rented an apartment in Reading, then later moved to Laureldale and opened a small hardware store with garages on Marian Street. They lived there until 1942 when they bought a roughly 40-acre farm in Alsace Township near the town of Oley, which remained their home for the rest of their lives.

By this time, Midget cars had become very popular. Midgets were so popular Hollywood had Mickey Rooney racing one in the movies, and St. Louis Cardinal Dizzy Dean was only one of several major league baseball players to own one. In 1936 Hinnershitz got a ride in Harvey Tatersall's car for a race at the Madison Square Garden Bowl in New York City. For the next three years, Hinnershitz followed a busy schedule of Midget racing. During this period, most tracks featuring the Midgets were wood or paved. Soon he was racing in Midgets at the Nutley, New Jersey, Velodrome, a 1/7-mile high banked board track that had been built for bicycle racing, at another famous board track in Altoona, Pennsylvania, and at Philadelphia's paved 1/5 mile Yellow Jacket Speedway, which was located at Erie Avenue and G Street in Philadelphia.

However, racing on dirt is what he really wanted to do. He worked hard to develop a driving style he could use effectively on dirt—getting the car sideways, using the right gearing and tires, working the throttle, and using steady steering to get through the turns up against the outside fence while maintaining high speed to come off the turns fast. Few other drivers could do it, and Hinnershitz realized he had mastered a special technique. So he quit racing Midgets. His last Midget ride was in 1939. From that time on he raced Sprint cars and occasionally Championship cars on dirt except for his three starts in the Indianapolis 500 and a few other rare occasions.

Also in 1936, good fortune came his way. Hinnershitz was hired to drive the Gus Strupp 220 Miller Sprint car, a first-class piece of equipment. Strupp's regular driver Johnny Hannon, the 1934 AAA Eastern Sprint Car Champion, whose hometown was Norristown, Pennsylvania, was killed the year before in a Championship car during practice at Indianapolis. The car he died in was repaired and given to Clay Weatherly, who qualified it. On the ninth lap of the 1935 Indianapolis 500, Weatherly went out over the northwest wall and was killed.

With Hannon now dead, Strupp put Bob Sall in his car; then he tried Ben Shaw and later Floyd Roberts. All three were talented drivers. These were the days before power steering, and the Strupp car had a reputation for demanding a little bit more strength to handle. Roberts seemed to do the best, but he gave up the ride. Roberts won at Indianapolis in 1938 and was killed there in 1939 defending his title. Later it was reported that Hannon had directed that if something happened to him, Gus was to give the ride to Hinnershitz. Strupp was impressed with Hinnershitz, so he put him in the car for the 1936 season, and he had a successful season driving it.

Hinnershitz kept busy in 1937, racing a full schedule of Sprint cars and Midgets for various car owners, frequently driving Sex Perriman's Sprint car.

At the start of the 1938 season, Hinnershitz was driving for Light and later for Johnny Gerber, a dirt track racer through and through from Iowa. Gerber was a driver, mechanic, chassis and engine builder, and race-team owner. Maynard "Hungry" Clark usually drove Gerber's back-up car.

The Gerber team had a huge hog as a mascot that was always tied up near their pit. The hog served as a reminder to everyone that the team's nickname was "The Iowa Pig Farmers." One of Gerber's other peculiarities was his preference for running racecars bob-tail, that is, without the tail section. AAA officials, including retired driver and 1912 Indianapolis 500 winner Joe Dawson, enforced the mandatory tail section rule, frequently citing Gerber for violating it. Gerber decided to give up driving and concentrate on running the team and serving as chief mechanic. He kept Clark on as the team's main driver. Gerber had a lot of outlaw in him; his racecars were not pretty. A bystander in the pits would stop and look in awe at what appeared to be a piece of junk. But then Clark would climb in it and set fast time and give a good beating to the competition. Hinnershitz signed on as a member of the "Iowa Hog Farmers," usually driving the main Gerber car. It appeared that good things were on the horizon when on September 25, 1938 he won his first feature race at the Reading Fairgrounds. Bad luck made a quick return three days later when he slid off the boards at the Nutley Velodrome in a Midget race and landed upside down. He escaped serious injury.

A turning point in Tommy Hinnershitz's career would come at the end of 1939. That's when he met "Mr. Auto-racing"—Ted Horn.

Chapter 2

Ted Horn
and Gasoline Alley, New Jersey

Ted Horn, born Eylard Theodore Von Horn on February 27, 1910, in Cincinnati, Ohio, probably had more influence on the career of Tommy Hinnershitz than any other person. Hinnershitz learned how to really drive racecars from Ted Horn, who had more than once been a houseguest at the Hinnershitz farm.

When Horn was a child, he moved with his family to Los Angeles. When he was 15 years old, he got a job at the *Los Angeles Times*. Later, as the story goes, instead of getting fined when he was stopped for speeding, the cop impounded his car and told him to go to the local speedway and get speeding out of his system. It turned out the racetrack had more racecars than it had drivers, so instead of Horn getting speeding out of his system, he got the chance to race.

He quickly launched his career, racing primarily at Legion Ascot Speedway and learning to drive by following the advice of other drivers. A short time later, he received serious injuries—burns to his back and a broken foot. He persisted and soon became friends with the legendary driver and engine-builder Louis Meyer. Horn headed to the Midwest and eventually east, traveling to more and more racetracks where he could learn from the experienced men inventing the sport.

Horn based his racing operations at Gasoline Alley in Paterson, New Jersey, a block of rented garages located at 29th Street between 17th and 18th avenues and anchored by Willie Belmont's tavern nearby at 31st and Market streets. Drivers, owners, mechanics, and car builders such as Roscoe "Pappy" Hough began their careers at the tavern.

Hough had the rare talent to tinker with resulting innovation. He is one of the men whose ingenuity and labor rubbed off on his rivals at the racetrack and those based in the alley, and as a result, helped steer the sport to where it went and is today.

Born in Paterson in November 1902, Hough won races in most of the fifty states and in three foreign countries. He made over 500 starts in racecars of all kinds, winning a NASCAR (National Association of Stock Car Racing) Short Track Division Championship in 1951. He's mostly known, however, as a Midget car owner.

"Pappy" owned a five Midget car team, nicknamed the "Five Little Pigs." Often racing seven days a week all over the Northeast, the cars were towed from track to track on a double-decked trailer. They were among Hinnershitz's fiercest competitors during that prime Midget racing period with the frantic race schedules during the late 1930s. The team raced on dirt ovals, short tracks, road courses, and the Nutley Velodrome banked board track, where they were challenged by rival Tommy Hinnershitz, who came over from Pennsylvania.

In 1951 Pappy decided to give NASCAR a try. His racecar-driving with that organization lasted four years. But NASCAR came into existence too late for him to develop a long-term record. When his days as a driver came to an end during the 1950s, he continued to build racecars at Gasoline Alley. He never retired, working in his garage day and night until his death in 1995 at the age of 92.

In the 1930s and 1940s, car owners would bring their damaged cars to Paterson for repairs. Racing mechanics, drivers, pit crewmembers, and owners found common ground at Gasoline Alley. There they could work on their cars, help one another and just hang around while discussing the latest auto-racing news. Frankie DelRoy worked there. The short and lightweight ex-riding mechanic, who worked with Offenhauser engineering and was a Kurtis Kraft dealer, sold components and complete Midget racecars. DelRoy went on to become a successful chief mechanic at Indianapolis.

Ted Horn surrounded himself with these people. Throughout the 1934 season, while campaigning in Sprint car events, he attracted the attention of engine builder Harry Miller. Miller and Preston Tucker were working on a project with Ford Motor Company for the 1935 Indianapolis 500. Tucker, a visionary born in 1903, is famous for his radically innovative 1948 Tucker automobile. He was accused of stock fraud in 1949, resulting in the production of the car being shut down. Many of the features on the Tucker are widely used on modern automobiles. In 1988 a major motion picture, *Tucker: The Man and His Dream*, was released. Miller hired Horn to drive one of the new Miller Ford V8 cars. Horn qualified the car but dropped out with steering problems after 145 laps.

Horn considered his performance for Miller a failure. However, car owner Harry Hartz, a former driver, was impressed enough to give Horn a ride for the 1936 Indianapolis 500. Hartz sought to teach the young driver how to drive at Indianapolis, and Horn, eager to learn, followed his instructions. They quickly became a serious threat to win the Indianapolis 500. Horn finished second in his first race with Hartz. He raced two more times with Hartz at Indianapolis, finishing third in 1937 and fourth in 1938.

He went on to finish fourth in 1939 and again in 1940, and third in 1941. When auto-racing resumed in 1945, Horn won all seven races he entered that year. The next three years were very successful; he won the national championship for three consecutive years—1946, 1947, and 1948. Victory at Indianapolis eluded him, but he did finish in the top four positions nine consecutive times.

In late 1939 or early 1940, Horn asked Hinnershitz to join his T.H.E. (Ted Horn Enterprises) racing team. Hinnershitz's memory during interviews in later years couldn't pinpoint the exact date he came on board. The exact date is lost to history; it was probably discussed over weeks or months before Hinnershitz first climbed into one of the first class T.H.E. Sprint cars. Back at Gasoline Alley, Horn had garages full of Sprint cars and plenty of money to race and maintain them.

It was the break Hinnershitz needed. Horn was a very talented driver and a good teacher. Hinnershitz learned by listening, watching, and following his boss. His ability to learn and adapt quickly would carry him throughout his career. On September 12, 1948, Hinnershitz beat his boss at Williams Grove. It was the only Sprint car defeat for Horn in 1948.

Horn was killed on the second lap in a Championship car race at DuQuoin, Illinois, on October 10, 1948. According to reports at the time, one of the front spindles collapsed, causing the front axle to dig into the racetrack. Had Horn's crew known that the kingpin was flapping up and down because of wear either to the kingpin or the shaft holding it, the accident might have been prevented. Either the kingpin popped out the top or dropped out of the bottom of the shaft. After Horn's death, mechanics began drilling two small holes and bridging a piece of wire across the top of the shaft that holds the kingpin. If the kingpin moved up and down as a result of wear or defect, it would clearly tear through the bridge made with the piece of wire. Between events, the pit crew could quickly and easily check if the wire was still in place and if it was, be assured that the kingpin was tight and snugly fit.

At the time of the tragic accident, Horn had already clinched the 1948 Championship Division title and Eastern Sprint car title. He is buried at Cedar Lawn Cemetery at Lakeview and Crook Avenues in Paterson, New Jersey. He was survived by wife Gerry and four daughters, Loretta, Theresa, Kathy, and Gayeleen.

Chapter 3

The American Automobile Association

While racecar drivers made heroes of themselves on the racetracks, master race promoter Ralph Hankinson made them heroes in the press. There was a time when the average Sprint car fan only got to see one automobile race per year; that race was at the local county fair.

You can only go around a half-mile dirt track so fast; the Sprint cars of today are doing it just seconds faster than they did 50 years ago. When that fact is considered, the racecar drivers of the *early years* are even more respected. They raced with far less sophisticated equipment when compared to the engines, chassis, and tires that are used today on modern, improved track surfaces. Hinnershitz and his contemporaries of those *early years* had to invent, innovate, design, and engineer practically everything used to build and compete a racecar. Before they could make anything, they had to make the patterns. They built race engines from hunks of metal. Their early technology made modern automobile racing what it is today.

For most of the first half of the 20th century, the AAA Contest Board controlled championship American automobile racing. Most people today know AAA as a travel agency and a club that offers an assortment of services to motorists. At the time of its founding, competition was an important part of supporting automobile owners. In 1908 AAA stepped into the then chaotic world of auto-racing and formed a contest board to organize it.

After the Indianapolis Motor Speedway began running 500-mile races in 1911, the track came to dominate racing in the United States and soon the contest board itself. Eddie Rickenbacker was both president of the speedway and chairman of the contest board. AAA soon came to control the best drivers and promoters and, in the process, became arbitrary and overbearing. AAA made a lot of enemies. Creating more rules increased the amount of policing that was needed, and creating more opportunities for officials to mete out fines and suspensions was part of the effort to increase AAA's ever tightening control on auto-racing. Many AAA rules were actually comical. AAA had at one time, with the cooperation of the Indianapolis Motor Speedway, required all drivers to check in their false teeth with officials. That rule was enacted as an attempt to reduce serious mouth injuries.

An example of the arrogance was the board's refusal to sanction a race at the Michigan State Fairgrounds in 1914 because an unsanctioned Midget race had been held there. The fair board became so enraged they teamed up with other fairs and various promoters to form the very successful IMCA (International Motor Contest Association). AAA considered IMCA and anybody associated with the organization "outlaws." This AAA derogatory term describes almost every Sprint car owner and driver racing during the *modern years*. IMCA continues to operate as a successful organization.

During the 1920s and 30s, AAA ruled championship racing, including the Indianapolis 500, and practically all of Sprint car racing. Uncooperative and disobedient drivers were harshly disciplined. Fines were imposed, and suspensions were a major obstacle for drivers hoping to race in the Indianapolis 500. A challenge to AAA's authority was the advent of the newly popular Midgets in 1933 and the founding of the Midget sanctioning club ARDC (American Race Drivers Club) in 1939. But through its control of the Indianapolis 500, AAA was able to continue its control of the sport because starting in the Indianapolis 500 was the ultimate goal of practically every *champion*.

It lasted until 1956 when AAA abruptly pulled out of automobile racing, replaced by the hastily organized USAC by Indianapolis Motor Speedway owner Tony Hullman and others. The reason AAA gave for quitting was the ever-increasing criticism it was receiving because of the deaths and injuries so prevalent in auto-racing at the time.

Perhaps the straw that broke the camels back was the 1955 Le Mans disaster on June 11, 1955, during the 24 Hours of LeMans. A racecar got involved in an accident and careened into a crowd of spectators. Racecar driver Pierre Levegh and 80 spectators were killed. It is considered the most catastrophic accident in auto-racing history.

Chapter 4

The Promoters

Like in these present *modern days*, drivers, owners, and mechanics traveled all over the country competing for high stakes during the *early years*. During this period, drivers died regularly every year; the smells of death and injury were always in the air. These were the days of high speed with no seat belts, roll bars, or cages to protect a driver while his car flipped violently. A spinning racecar, unseen through the thick dust by the 20 or so drivers charging from behind, could cause devastating wreckage and injury. The fans waited the entire year to see the famous speeding daredevils like Ted Horn, Joie Chitwood, Walt Ader, Billy Arnold, Fred Frame, Lee Wallard, and the Pennsylvania Dutchman Tommy Hinnershitz in their racecars with the engines whining loudly. It was race day at the fair complete with the high school band, visiting dignitaries, and a track announcer capable of building up every fan's enthusiasm. A backlog of cars along the highway waiting to park acres away and long lines at the ticket window were all part of the race day ritual.

For overweight and squeaky-voiced Ralph A. Hankinson, 1924 was a bad year. It was so bad his wife had to go back to performing her circus wire act she did before they were married. Ralph "Pappy" Hankinson was a race promoter, booking races at fairs through George Hamid and his booking agency. Hamid was also a former circus performer who eventually owned circuses, amusement midways, the famous Steel Pier in Atlantic City, New Jersey, and the Trenton Speedway and New Jersey State Fairgrounds in Trenton, New Jersey.

When racing seasons were over, Hankinson and his family usually spent winters in Florida; however, during the winter of 1926-27, the Hankinsons lived at the Cadillac Hotel in New York City. It was here that the 1927 racing season was planned. The first thing Hankinson did was negotiate an agreement with AAA to sanction his races. It greatly improved his chances of financial success.

It was Hamid's job to try to book races into fairgrounds that he was already conducting business with at the time. The next problem for Hankinson to solve was getting enough drivers to compete. Because the fair season was so short, Hankinson needed to run races at three different fairs in one day to make a profit. He went to Langhorne where that town's one-mile dirt track had opened two years earlier, to sign up drivers. Virtually all the drivers he signed became famous in AAA. Among them were Ray Keech, Zeke Meyers, Doc MacKenzie, and Johnny Hannon. In all, during the 1927 season, Hankinson ran 41 AAA sanctioned races, almost half of all the races AAA sanctioned that year, the most they had ever sanctioned in one season.

On October 15, 1927, racecar driver Floyd Samuel Nunis—they called him Sam—was hurt at Concord, North Carolina. After he recovered from his injuries, Hankinson hired Nunis to work the promotional part of the organization. It would launch a long career for Nunis as a public relations master and race promoter. Later he settled down with his family in the Kenhorst section of Reading.

In 1928 Hankinson got more drivers to come east and race at the fairs he had under contract. He was looking for famous drivers who would draw fans into the grandstands. This new group of drivers included Fred Frame, Billy Arnold, and Ralph DePalma. That year Hankinson ran fewer races, dropping the financial losers, which reduced costs and the hard workload while lessening the constant flow of problems inherent to the entertainment business. While decreasing the number of the organization's problems, cash was still tight, and AAA couldn't find enough officials to cover all the races.

Finally the contest board hired Dawson, Vince Tully, and Shorty Pritzbur. These three men, among others, brought stability to rules enforcement. They also set up an office in the South to officiate Hankinson's Southern fair dates.

The following year Arnold helped ticket sales when he began terrorizing all the dirt tracks on which he raced. Reportedly, he was the first man to circle the Reading Fairgrounds' half-mile track in less than 30 seconds, timed at 29.20 seconds.

In May 1930, Hankinson promoted his first race at Langhorne Speedway with an all-star field, including superstar DePalma. Hoping to repeat the success of the May race, he came back and promoted an October event. Frank Farmer won that day, with Herman Schurch setting a new track record of 36.40. Swiss-born Schurch was killed the following year on November 10, 1931, during warmups at the half-mile dirt track at Ascot Park, California. By the time the 1930 season ended, Hankinson had money again and paid off all the debts he incurred during his lean years. Hamid gave him an office in New York, and they began working as a team.

In 1931 Hankinson's true "carnie" character showed. Just as P. T. Barnum had brought singer Jenny Lind, dubbed the "Swedish Nightingale," to America for a successful tour in the late 19th century, Hankinson brought a French woman racecar driver to America who had won Grand Prix races in France and other European countries. Her name was Hekle Nice. Of course, AAA wouldn't let her race so Hankinson booked her as a special fair attraction trying to set track records dressed in all white and driving an all-white car. Fans talked about Nice for years.

Never one to rest, Hankinson leased the Altoona Speedway and ran the last two races there on the board track. The boards were so warped and rotted small flags were placed at all the track's holes.

The Hankinson organization experienced another good year in 1932. Race events were held as far west and north as Huron, South Dakota, and Ottawa, Canada. The organization by now had become a well-oiled machine, managed with efficiency from its offices at 151 North Fifth Street in Reading. Advance men produced all the publicity, sold ads in the race program, and churned out the organization's own racing paper sold at every race. During the winter,

Hankinson bought Langhorne Speedway, planning to run one race before Indianapolis and one after.

During the 1934 season, Hankinson made a prediction that wasn't taken lightly, considering he set standards for promoting Sprint car racing that are used to this day. He predicted a bright future for a young, upcoming and talented driver named Tommy Hinnershitz. He knew the kid had only earned 80 points in the Hankinson Sprint Circuit, finishing 63rd in the standings, but he had seen enough racing and racecar drivers to recognize talent and potential when he saw it. Hinnershitz competed in Hankinson races in Pennsylvania at Schuylkill Haven, Reading, Hughesville, and Langhorne, and in New Jersey at Flemington and Hohokus. He had raced the Jules Furslew owned car, a flathead that wasn't in the same class as cars being driven by Billy Winn, Mackenzie, Hannon and others, but he made do. Hinnershitz was destined for a successful career, competing under the Hankinson banner produced by a man and his staff who seemed to invent some new aspect of Sprint car racing every day. Hankinson, over the course of his career, made it possible for drivers and owners to compete; he entertained hundreds of thousands of people and helped non-profit fair boards raise millions of dollars.

In the winter of 1934, Hankinson signed up the Illinois, Wisconsin, and New York State Fairs, and then quickly recognized he needed to get more drivers. He sent Nunis and Bob Sall to California. Sall befriended a young driver named Ted Horn while Nunis signed up Al Gordon, Rex Mays, Roberts, and several others to come back and race at the Eastern fairs. On the way home, Nunis and Sall stopped to visit promoter Frank Funk who had some good drivers running with him at his track in Winchester, Indiana. While they were visiting Funk, Nunis signed up Tony Bettenhausen, Spider Webb, Duke Dinsmore, Wilbur Shaw, and a few more. While the drivers were being signed, Hankinson expanded his publicity staff, adding Pat Purcell and Gaylord White, along with Russ Moyer. Moyer was new to auto-racing; he eventually became the long-time race director for the Reading Fair. The Hankinson circuit lost two drivers at the end of the season, not tragically this time. DePalma retired from racing and Frame got a good job with Ford Motor Company.

Another big year came in 1935. In the spring, Hinnershitz

switched from AAA to running "outlaw." Mark Light re-opened the old Lebanon Fairgrounds horse track in Lebanon, and began promoting Sprint car racing on the half-mile. Using the name "Tommy Milton" to hide his identity from AAA and prevent fines, Hinnershitz won his first career feature at Lebanon on April 13, 1935, in a car owned by Light. Hinnershitz came back two weeks later to grab a second in the feature. It had been convenient racing at Lebanon under Light's promotion because there was no long traveling. Lebanon was only about 35 miles from Hinnershitz's house.

Cautious Hinnershitz thought it was time to stop confusing AAA officials. He suspected Dawson knew all along he was running outlaw, so it was just a matter of time before punishment would be meted out. Hinnershitz's outlaw activity was allowed to go on for a little while until the inevitable warning, which luckily came from the benevolent pro-driver Dawson.

The real Tommy Milton had won the 1921 and 1923 Indianapolis 500, starting from the pole. Perhaps choosing to use Milton's name was out of respect for his resolve to achieve victory. In 1920 Milton had shown up at the sands of Daytona with his mechanic Jimmy Murphy in a duel engine Duesenberg. Milton then left to race in Cuba and asked Murphy to test run the car. Murphy had his practice run timed and set a world record practice run. Milton was outraged when he returned. He fired Murphy and then set up a tent to rebuild both engines that had sucked up sand during Murphy's run. In April Milton built up speed for four miles and then entered the measured mile. The car caught fire, but Milton didn't stop until he set a new record of 156.046 miles per hour. The whole car was on fire as Milton drove it into the ocean to douse the flames. The following year, Murphy became the first American to win a European auto race and then went on to victory in the French Grand Prix at Le Mans.

After a couple of those outlaw races, Hinnershitz returned to AAA competition. His first start was at Reading where he had a spectacular crash in a car owned by Herb Kauffman. After driving some other racecars, he got the ride in Light's Miller, a car good enough to enable him to run up front. Things were starting to look better.

Meanwhile, Horn got his first ride at Indianapolis in a car built for Edsel Ford by Harry Miller. Horn dropped out of the race with steering problems. Hankinson's good relationship with Indianapolis Speedway had cleared the path for Horn.

To wrap up the 1935 season, Hankinson promoted an October race at Atlanta, Georgia, before traveling to Florida with Major E. B. Allen of the Flemington Fair. Hankinson wanted to buy a hotel in Florida to run during the winter. He bought one in Orange City. The Atlanta race, run on the one-mile dirt track at Lakewood Park, was a success. Hinnershitz finished third in the first heat but was forced out of the 25-lap feature. The following month he married Betty Selman in Lebanon.

At the end of the year, Hinnershitz finished 10th in points in the Hankinson Circuit, accumulating 905 points, and finished 13th in the Eastern AAA Sprint Circuit with 361 points. He ended the season 16th in the Central Pennsylvania Sprint Circuit standings with 73 points.

In 1936 Hankinson bought Horn a racecar. It was the first car Horn ever owned. He finished second in the Indianapolis 500, and the first thing he did was pay Hankinson back

Because Indianapolis Motor Speedway president Eddie Rickenbacker was getting involved with Eastern Airlines and had little time to spend on auto-racing, the speedway's management approached Hankinson about taking over the reigns of the track. The brick track had fallen on hard times during the depression. Hankinson turned down the offer. Was that one of his mistakes? He would have had to give up Langhorne Speedway and all the other promotions in which his organization was involved, including all the fair dates, to have the time and resources needed to run the speedway. Hankinson might have suspected the speedway would follow the path of the board tracks and eventually fail.

With the 1936 season winding down, the Springfield, Illinois, and Milwaukee, Wisconsin, fair races were all set. It was a grueling weekend. After the race on Saturday, August 22, at Springfield, there was the long tow to Milwaukee to race on Sunday. The Springfield race was the first time MacKenzie raced since being hurt at Reading back in April. Hinnershitz had won the first heat that day at Reading and finished fourth in the 40-lap feature. MacKenzie didn't perform

L to R: Ted Horn, seated in racecar, "Thommy" Thomas, and famed chief mechanic Frankie Delroy pictured at Milwaukee, Wisconsin in 1946.

Armin Krueger/Greenfield Studio Photo

Ted Horn in 1938

Armin Krueger/Greenfield Studio Photo

Tommy Hinnershitz in his Bluebird Offy, built by Bob Blake, at Milwaukee, Wisconsin, in 1949

Armin Krueger/Greenfield Studio Photo

Tommy Hinnershitz poses in his Miracle Power Special at the Reading, Pennsylvania Fairgrounds circa 1953.

Miracle Power Products Corporation photo

Auto-racing pioneer Cyrus Patschke competed in the first Indianapolis 500 in 1911.

Photo courtesy of Pennsylvania Sports Hall of Fame

Joie Chitwood in 1941

Armin Krueger/Greenfield Studio Photo

Mark Light in 1949

Armin Krueger/Greenfield Studio Photo

Ottis Stine at Williams Grove Speedway, Mechanicsburg, Pennsylvania in 1952

From the Carl Sweigart collection

Mike Nazaruk poses at Indianapolis Motor Speedway before the start of the 1954 race. He finished 5th.

Armin Krueger/Greenfield Studio Photo

Johnnie Parsons is shown winning the rain-shortened 1950 Indianapolis 500 in the same car Tommy Hinnershitz drove to a 9th-place finish in the 1948 race.

Armin Krueger/Greenfield Studio Photo

Bill Holland, 1949 Indianapolis 500 winner, in the Blue Crown Spark Plug Special

Armin Krueger/Greenfield Studio Photo

Johnny Thomson at Williams Grove Speedway, Mechanicsburg, Pennsylvania circa 1953.

From the Carl Sweigart collection

Floyd Delp, car owner and Red Riegel's business partner, poses with his new Sprint car in 1953.

From the Delp Family collection

well at Springfield, and the next day at Milwaukee he was killed in the first lap of the race.

Roberts had been in the accident at Reading with MacKenzie. They both spent time in the Reading Hospital. During the hospital stay, MacKenzie married his fiancée Verna Mather, with Roberts serving as the "best man." On his wedding day, MacKenzie had just 38 days to live.

The 1936 season ended abruptly for Hinnershitz. While running in his last race of the year at Danbury, Connecticut, he rolled the Strupp Miller after losing a wheel. He was thrown from the car and suffered a leg injury.

He had tallied 902 AAA Sprint car points, finishing second in the standings. He finished fourth in the Hankinson standings with 1470 points. Hinnershitz had become a serious contender.

Hankinson and his organization kept busy during the 1937 and 1938 seasons, running the fair dates and Langhorne Speedway.

During 1937 Hankinson spent about $65,000 on his Florida hotel that was built in 1880. On December 15, 1937, he opened the beautifully remodeled resort after borrowing about $25,000 from Hamid to cover start-up expenses. It was one of the biggest mistakes he ever made. He used the hotel as a playground for fair people and racecar owners, drivers, and mechanics. Most were invited to stay as his guest, especially each February during the Florida State Fair in Tampa, starting up another auto-racing tradition. At times there wasn't a paying guest in the place, but he considered his generosity a gesture of good will and good business. He sent sports editors of newspapers $250 coupons to be used at the hotel during the summer and fall.

Since 1937 had been a good year, any time Hankinson heard that someone was coming to Florida, he would invite him or her and their families to the hotel for complimentary red carpet treatment. Good times got even better when Roy Richwine, owner of Williams Grove Amusement Park, came to Hankinson and asked him to design a racetrack for the park. After it was built, Hankinson and Richwine agreed not to run on competing dates or try to lure drivers from the other.

By 1938 Hankinson had become involved in other entertainment business ventures. He was busy saving financially-strapped fairs and promoting carnival acts. Buying the hotel in Florida had been a major mistake; however, he was about to make another that seemed insignificant at the time but eventually became the biggest mistake of his life. A Florida rookie promoter was given a contract by the city of Daytona Beach to produce a Fourth of July auto race. The city had lost $20,000 producing the race in 1936, and the local Elks Club lost a substantial amount of money when it tried promoting the race in 1937. The rookie, a racecar mechanic and driver living in a $13.50-a-month rented bungalow, was worried because he had no experience as a promoter. He had the contract, but he wasn't sure whether he could pull it off. He couldn't spare the 25 cents for a long distance phone call, so he decided to place a collect call to the famous veteran promoter Ralph Hankinson for help. Hankinson refused to accept the call. Undeterred, the rookie found another partner named Charlie Reese, a saloon owner with a less than ideal reputation, to help promote what turned out to be a successful and financially rewarding race. Later Reese would opt out and mysteriously disappear. What was the rookie promoter's name? Bill France, Sr. The rest is NASCAR history.

More misfortune came Hankinson's way during 1938. He began experiencing trouble with AAA. In Springfield at the Illinois State Fair, so many cars broke down, and along with the death of Billy Winn, Hankinson went to Milwaukee with only 15 cars. Ralph Ammund, head of the Wisconsin State Fair, told Hankinson how unhappy he was. Ammund, who had just been elected to the AAA Board of Directors, immediately canceled the Hankinson organization out of Milwaukee for 1939. Additionally, the fair in Springfield now required that he run a 100-mile Championship car race. Since 1936 it had been a Sprint car race. AAA made matters worse when they told him they wouldn't issue a sanction unless it was for a Championship car race. AAA backed down, and the race was run only after Hankinson threatened to go to another association for the sanction.

The 1939 season started with opening day at Reading, where it had been held for the past nine years. Chitwood was attracting large crowds to the races mostly because he was portrayed as part Native American, which he wasn't. Sam Nunis had been doing track announcing for Montgomery Ward's Riverside Tires, covering races coast to coast. Nunis told Hankinson about Joie Chitwood, a talented young driver from out west. Hankinson quickly signed him; he was always looking for new talent. Chitwood was a new addition to an already impressive roster of drivers including Bill Holland, Ted Horn, Walt Brown, Mark Light, Lee Wallard, Ottis Stine, and a young developing driver named Tommy Hinnershitz. The 1939 season went along without a hitch. Joie Chitwood raced to the Hankinson Circuit championship in the beautiful Hank O'Day Sprint car, and was crowned AAA Eastern champion.

The 1940 season also got underway with the inaugural race at Reading. Just before the season's opener, Hankinson sold Langhorne Speedway to thrill show owner and performer Lucky Teeter for $65,000. AAA had been pressuring Hankinson to produce long distance championship races at Langhorne, but he kept resisting. He considered long races at the track too tiring and dangerous. But the main reason he sold the speedway was to help alleviate some of the debt he had acquired opening his Florida hotel.

The big attraction of the 1940 season was unquestionably Chitwood. Fans flocked to see the "Indian" do his daredevil antics behind the wheel. But Chitwood didn't have it easy. In fact, it was Hinnershitz in the O'Day car on September 6, 1940, when he flipped it at Rutland, Vermont, while taking time, receiving serious injuries to his right arm. Hinnershitz, along with Horn, Sall, Tony Willman, Bill Holland, and others, gave Chitwood a serious run.

All throughout 1940, AAA was having serious problems with the Championship car division. Finding places to run races and having enough cars showing up were both continuing problems. AAA desperately tried to keep enough cars active so it would have a full field to run the Indianapolis 500. Without Indianapolis, it is probable AAA would have stopped sanctioning races at that time. The association's priority had become offering an assortment of services to motorists and establishing a travel agency business. The situation became so desperate it bought cars to enter in the Indianapolis 500.

Friction continued between AAA and Hankinson. One of the problems was AAA didn't want to run the small county fair tracks that could only afford small purses. Hankinson felt these small fairs that supported him over the years should have auto-racing. He began booking these dates but turned them over to people who worked for him, especially Nunis. The purses were small, but every driver who appeared got paid some money.

The AAA reluctantly continued sanctioning these races, classifying them as "Class B" events. The only reason AAA maintained a presence was the fear an "outlaw" sanctioning body would come in and get a foothold. AAA's priority was to get as much money as they could from the fair boards. Hankinson didn't operate that way. Honest and always paying the drivers and car owners well, he charged the fair boards what they could afford to pay and gave the fans the best show the available money could buy.

After AAA made the decision to discipline Hankinson for helping to promote an "outlaw" event, it was apparent that AAA and Hankinson's differences meant they were no longer going to be able to work together. In late 1940, Hankinson severed all ties with AAA. He signed an agreement with CSRA (Central States Racing Association) to sanction his races. At the end of the 1940 season, Hankinson tried to get Horn to run with him during 1941, but Horn wasn't going to jeopardize his good standing with AAA and lose eligibility to race in the 1941 Indianapolis 500. Hankinson also tried to sign Rex Mays and Mauri Rose, but neither of them could make any plans because they had commitments related to the threat of war.

Over the previous years, CSRA had raced in Pennsylvania at Bird-In-Hand, Lebanon, Lehighton, Landisville, Hughesville, Clearfield, Bedford, and other smaller tracks. Many of the racecars were homebuilt, and some were crude and primitive. Drivers usually received only local recognition. Among the drivers who raced with CSRA were Dutch Culp, Al Gasta, Johnny Zohner, Paul Young, Dutch Shollenberger, Ammon Kelcher, and Dave Wilt. Some former CSRA drivers that went on to great careers include Hinnershitz, Light, Stine, and Ted Nyquist.

Hankinson had been involved with auto-racing beginning in 1910 and was associated with AAA from 1927 until 1940. Now the possibility of war, and all the uncertainties that go along with it, was disrupting his auto race promoting. Hankinson died at his hotel in Florida on August 19, 1942, just a few weeks after auto-racing ceased because of World War II.

After the war, Nunis took over the Hankinson operation. He had learned the business from the master, and now he had his chance to be not just a race promoter; it was his opportunity to be a showman. Nunis had begun to make his own mark mostly because he had original ideas that drew crowds and pleased the fans. One of his innovations that continues to be a part of American auto-racing is the inverted start, where the slower cars that took time trials start up front in the heat races. As part of the qualifying process, time trials are where a driver has normally two laps to run under the clock and the faster of these two laps is his qualifying time. The qualifying time determines where a car and driver will start in the feature, or main event, but only if the driver qualifies in a heat, or preliminary race. In the feature event, the fastest cars start up front, and before the Nunis innovation, the same starting order applied for the heat races as well. This Nunis innovation gave some of the slower cars a chance to make the feature plus created a lot more passing while the faster cars raced up front to qualify. Nunis knew the more passing there is the happier the fans are.

Sam Nunis expertly did business with corporate executives, local government officials, fair board members, drivers, car owners, mechanics, and race officials. He tended to every detail. The job of race promoter has always been challenging. How many hot dogs to cook, how much ice to buy, how many security guards to hire, personally supervising track preparation, buying advertising, selling ads in the program book, writing and printing news releases, and hiring good advance men and a decent announcer is just a partial list of things a promoter must do. For Hankinson, and now Nunis, sometimes the money was good and sometimes there wasn't any money left after paying the bills. On some occasions there wasn't enough money to pay the bills. But the tall and skinny Nunis enjoyed the work. He was doing what he always wanted to do; he was in show business. Auto-racing, especially at state and county fairs, was then and still is indeed show business.

Born on December 16, 1900, in Esom Hill, Alabama, Nunis left town at age 16, running off to Birmingham. He hopped freight trains and eventually found himself in Detroit working at the Ford factory. Just after World War I, he first saw the early version of the Hankinson auto-racing show; in that version, Hankinson owned all the cars, and the winner was pre-arranged. Running that type of auto-racing, actually an exhibition, was called "hippodroming." Nunis was captivated by what he saw. He asked Hankinson for a job driving one of the racecars but was turned down. He quit the Ford job and started hanging around Hankinson and his troupe, tagging along from town to town on his own. He finally got hired and stayed a couple of years. After crashing one of the cars and spending 18 months in recovery, which included a metal plate installed in his hip, Hankinson took him on as one of his assistants.

Later Nunis took a job with Montgomery Ward's Riverside Tires in sales promotion, eventually becoming East Coast representative. Riverside Tires were used by most of the dirt track racers, and the company was deeply involved in auto-racing promotions and sponsorships. Jack Story, IMCA's announcer at most races, had a radio show sponsored by Montgomery Ward. Through Jack, Nunis and Chitwood became friends, which led to a sponsorship that lasted several seasons.

When World War II started, Nunis enrolled in Montgomery Ward's corporate training program in Baltimore, but that job lasted only six months. He showed up at Gasoline Alley in Paterson, and on a whim bought the garages and Willie Belmont's tavern from Chitwood. He didn't realize at the time that alcoholic beverages were rationed. Nunis knew a con when he saw one. He unloaded the place in 1944. Despite that business deal, he and Chitwood remained friends for many years.

When the war ended Nunis returned to auto-racing, promoting races along the entire East Coast. He promoted the first race ever run at Selinsgrove, Pennsylvania, on Saturday afternoon, July 20, 1946, an AAA sanctioned event. Nunis had what it took to give upcoming drivers and new or neglected speedways the jumpstart they needed to be successful. Chitwood had designed the fast half-mile dirt Selinsgrove oval, purposely featuring a front stretch much wider than normal to provide a large area to host his thrill show. Bill Holland, who later went on to win the Indianapolis 500 in 1949, won the 20-lap inaugural event. Robert "Red" Byron, who placed second behind Holland, won NASCAR's first sanctioned beach race in 1948 and became NASCAR's first Grand National Champion in 1949.

After AAA pulled out of racing and NASCAR began moving into his territory, Nunis realized that he needed to concentrate on one track if he wanted to continue presenting championship auto-racing. He began working with showman Hamid. Nunis took over as promoter of Trenton Speedway featuring USAC Championship cars and NASCAR Grand National cars.

Eventually Nunis retired from Trenton, and despite health problems, did promote some URC (United Racing Club) races into the early 1970s. He died in 1980.

Chapter 5

A Neighborhood of Pioneers

With the advent of the automobile in the latter years of the 19th century and the eventual mass production in the early years of the 20th, auto-racing was born. It was a natural happening because those who engineered the first automobiles needed to test and experiment.

They were men who had nothing to copy from; there were no prototypes. There were no earlier versions of anything. Before they could make a part, they needed to make the pattern. Tommy Hinnershitz had watched some of this new breed of men race at Reading. They planted the seed of discontent in him that is essential for any racecar driver. Hinnershitz also came to realize early that men who surrounded him geographically were starting an automobile revolution that would eventually spread throughout the world.

The early geniuses of automobile building and racing were not all trained engineers, metallurgists, draftsmen, designers, and machinists. Actually, most of them were mechanics or welders; some were even left over blacksmiths who got involved because they knew how to heat up metal and bend it into particular shapes.

As automobiles became available to everyday people, these men began repairing them in their workshops called "garages." Automobiles became their livelihood, but they also wanted to have some fun. Racing that began as fun became a serious business for some. Those with little formal education, in particular, became the common-man innovators and inventors.

They built engines from a block of cast iron and hard metals. They became skilled at taking apart and putting back together again the Offenhauser engine, nicknamed the "Offy", that dominated Championship car and Sprint car racing for many years. They shaped sheet metal into beautiful covering, and they adapted the early automobile frames, brakes, wheels, and other necessary parts, into a racecar. Then they went to the salt flats, the horse track, or an open field to risk injury and financial loss for a chance at a little money, some fame and glory, and knowledge and know-how. While the automobile racing craze was spreading across America, efforts in California, or Indiana, or Florida, were miniscule when compared to Pennsylvania, and to a lesser extent New Jersey and New York. The history of Sprint car racing was written in Central and Eastern Pennsylvania.

Fans had an unquenchable thirst for Sprint cars and modified stock cars. Why the area surrounding Allentown, Reading, Lebanon, and Harrisburg, Pennsylvania, became such an incubator for auto-racing is not clearly evident. The area was bearing fruit years before favorite son *champion* Mario Andretti came along. Andretti, and others who have excelled in the sport locally, nationally, and internationally, helped assure that Pennsylvania auto-racing fans would develop and maintain an awesome love affair with auto-racing, prompting the advent of modified stock cars at local tracks throughout the East and the winged Sprint cars that race all over Central Pennsylvania.

Outsiders have always known that to win in Pennsylvania, you have to be extra good. Somewhere a seed was planted in enough Pennsylvania men's minds at about the same time to help create the sport of auto-racing. They were *neighbors*; almost all of them knew each other, some were friends, some were good friends, and some carried the rivalry to the depths of dislike. But they all seemed to be doing the same innovative things at the same time, some leading the way, especially the car builders and pioneers like Hinnershitz, who had that rare ability to transform a new idea into automotive reality. Some in the *neighborhood* did better than others, and beginning in those early years, even the mediocre could go west and win big time, starting a phenomenon that lives on into the 21st century.

Hinnershitz had these talented men as *neighbors* and rivals while he developed his talent as a racecar driver, owner, and mechanic. It helped to be enveloped in an atmosphere that enabled him to flourish on the track and in the garage. He appreciated in particular to have as *neighbors* close friend Johnny Thomson, whose farm was just a few miles to the east in Boyertown, and to the north in Allentown, master car builder Hiram Hillegass and his shop.

Another *neighbor*, who had his shop in the Riverside section of Reading, was friend Joe Wolfe. Wolfe specialized in high powered watercraft and owned the Championship car driven in the 1950 Indianapolis 500 by Joie Chitwood, who qualified the car in the 5th starting spot. Tony Bettenhausen, driving in relief, brought the car home 17th in the rain shortened 1950 race won by Johnnie Parsons. Parsons won the race in the very car Hinnershitz drove in the 1948 race.

Cyrus Patschke

A *neighbor* who preceded Hinnershitz, and maybe the man more responsible for founding the *neighborhood* than anyone else, was Cyrus Patschke, born July 6, 1888. He was inducted in to the Central Chapter of the Pennsylvania Sports Hall of Fame in 1974. Patschke, who owned a repair garage at 1101 Cumberland Street in Lebanon, is relatively unknown despite his considerable accomplishments in the sport.

A. Louden Snowden, a commissioner for Philadelphia's Fairmount Park at the turn of the 20th century, advocated a horse speedway, and within a few years, automobile races became a reality. For four years, early in the last century, auto-racing was run on an eight-mile course in the west section of the park that drew half a million spectators the first year. Unlike auto-racing at other locations, such as the Vanderbilt Cup races, there were never any serious injuries or deaths at Fairmount Park. Despite the safety record, racing was banned because of safety concerns.

There were protests demanding that auto-racing be brought back to the park. In fact, a campaign was started to build a two-mile oval, Philadelphia's attempt to compete with Indianapolis.

In June 1908, Patschke drove an Acme automobile in the races at

Jamaica, Long Island, winning both the two-mile and the one-mile events. In September at Fairmount Park, he finished second in the same car in a 195-mile race with a time of 4:14.54. In October he entered Brooklyn, New York's Brighton Beach 24-hour race. The Brighton Beach racetrack had been built in 1879 for horse and dog racing. Patschke and co-driver C. B. Rogers, again in the same Acme, dropped out after 11 hours

The next year, 1909, he won the Brighton Beach 24-hour race in a Lozier with teammate Ralph Mulford. Patschke returned the next year to win again with Al Poole in a Stearns-Six, believed to be the fastest stock automobile at the time. The Stearns cars were being built by F. B. Stearns Co. of Cleveland, Ohio. Frank Stearns, an early automotive pioneer, began building automobiles in 1896.

Patschke also raced at Point Breeze and competed in some of the Vanderbilt Cup races held in Nassua, Long Island between 1904 and 1910.

In 1910 he traveled to Indianapolis to help at the Marmon Racing Team factory run by Howard Marmon and Fred Moskowitz. As part of the Marmon team with drivers Ray Harroun and Joe Dawson, Patschke served as relief driver in the first Indianapolis 500. Near the halfway point in the race, Harroun turned the wheel over to Patschke, who drove the car for 87.5 miles, successfully working his way up through the field. Harroun returned for the final stint and won the very first Indianapolis 500 in a time of 6 hours and 42 minutes at an average speed of 74.602 miles per hour. Patschke also stepped in to help Dawson. Patschke didn't get the win and the glory that goes with it, but he received a share of the money. Because the Marmons were single seat cars, without a riding mechanic to look out the back for cars closing in, the Marmon team devised the first rear-view mirror ever used on a racecar or a passenger car.

In October Patschke finished second driving a Marmon on a road course in Santa Monica, California in an AAA sanctioned event. He raced two more times that year but failed to finish either event.

In 1914 Patschke finished third on the dirt oval at Sioux City, Iowa, again in a Marmon. Patschke only drove in 11 major races. He won three of them, finished second in one, and third in two of the events.

The people who visited the Patschke garage in Lebanon are testaments to Patschke's influence in auto-racing. He had by now become well-known nationally and internationally. Lebanon resident Francis Pence, who worked at the garage for seven years as a mechanic, told of the days Patschke's close friends Bill Barron, Pete DePaulo, Eddie Rickenbacher, Barney Oldfield, Wilbur Shaw, Dawson, and others would stop by when they were in the area.

Pence clearly remembered the day Henry Ford, Thomas Edison, and Andrew Mellon stopped for gas. Mellon was a founding member of the Mellon financial empire and later became United States Secretary of the Treasury under President Warren G. Harding. Pence said they were in Mellon's polished Packard and stopped by to see their friend Patschke on their way to a camp, presumably a hunting camp. Edison gave Pence a dollar and told him to go across the street to M. B. Maurer's store to buy ice cream cones.

Eventually Patschke's garage business included a Marmon automobile dealership. Marmon passenger cars, in the class of the Pierce Arrow, Peerless and Packard, were built and sold between the years of 1903 and 1933. Patschke died on May 6, 1951.

Mark Light

Later on, the tough competitor Mark Light had his garage just two blocks west of Patschke's, on the Southside of Cumberland Street in Lebanon, right in the middle of the *neighborhood*. The property is now used as residential apartments. Light was a successful driver, car owner, and promoter. His untidy workshop was legendary. A story—credible because so many local mechanics repeated it over the years—tells about the Pennsylvania State Trooper in charge of area auto-inspection stations giving Light an ultimatum—clean up the place or lose his inspection license. Light reached up and took the license off the wall and handed it to the cop.

Light's first venture as a promoter was to re-open the old Lebanon Fairgrounds' half-mile track, located one mile South of his garage. It was on this track in 1935 where Hinnershitz won his first feature race ever, racing under the name Tommy Milton.

Using the name Milton to cover-up his racing at non-sanctioned "outlaw tracks" brought a warning from AAA's Dawson at a race in

Delaware. Dawson, the 1912 Indianapolis 500 winner and 1911 Marmon team driver with Harroun and Patschke, was stern but also sympathetic to drivers. He could have fined or suspended Hinnershitz.

Hinnershitz went on to drive for Light numerous times over the next 15 years. Light was a good racecar driver in his own right, always fielding first-class equipment and racing against the best drivers of the day. He won an AAA Eastern Sprint car race at Langhorne Speedway in 1948, quite an accomplishment. He won the 1940 opener at Williams Grove and went on to be a five-time Sprint car feature winner there.

Light was one of Hinnershitz's best friends. Light's future wife June Plantz introduced her friend Betty to Hinnershitz. Betty Selman became Mrs. Tommy Hinnershitz.

Johnny Thomson

Hinnershitz was friends with many of his fellow drivers. He and Betty visited *neighbors* Johnny and Evie Thomson and their four sons in Boyertown, the next town over from Oley, in the eastern fringe of the *neighborhood*, just 10 miles away. Thomson, born April 9, 1922, and nicknamed "The Flying Scot," had won the 1954 AAA Eastern Sprint car championship and later the 1958 USAC Sprint car championship.

The decorated World War II veteran had become famous, finishing third in the Indianapolis 500. The Thomsons, who were originally from New England, settled on a farm in Boyertown to be closer to the hotbed of Eastern United States auto-racing.

Thomson got started racing Midgets, earning his first championship in 1948 after winning 32 features. He won his second title in 1950 and in 1952 won the AAA Eastern Midget championship.

By 1959 Thomson was established as a Championship and Sprint car driver, highlighted by the third-place finish at Indianapolis, finishing behind Jim Rathman and winner Rodger Ward. He had driven in the AAA and USAC Championship car series during the 1953-1960 seasons with 69 starts, including the Indianapolis 500 in each season. He finished in the top ten 43 times, with 7 victories. His chief mechanic for several Indianapolis starts was Roy Sherman, the first national Midget champion.

What set Thomson apart from the many great drivers like Billy Vukovich, Mike Nazaruk, and Jimmy Bryan, all who died racing, was the fact that they more or less stayed out of trouble until the crash that killed them. With Thomson, he seemed to crash more than he should have considering his enormous talent. The scheduled "Johnny Thomson Appreciation Day" at the Reading Fairgrounds was ruined because he couldn't be there. He was in the hospital with injuries suffered from flipping a Sprint car at Williams Grove.

Thomson forever left his mark at Langhorne because of his violent flip on June 19, 1955, that caused controversy. During the Championship car 100-mile race, he hit Jerry Hoyt, who had spun out after it began to rain on lap 45, in the fourth turn. Some made the accusation that Thomson hit Hoyt's stalled car while running full speed under caution. After Thomson hit Hoyt, his car flipped violently, going end over end several times out of the fourth turn and approaching the straightaway. He received severe injuries. Witnesses to the accident couldn't believe he lived through it. Jimmy Bryan went on to win the race.

On July 6, James Lamb, secretary of the AAA Contest Board, sent a letter from the AAA headquarters at 1712 G. Street, N. W., Washington, D. C., to Shorty Pritzbur, who was the chief steward of the race. Lamb wanted Pritzbur's opinion on whether Thomson was observing the yellow when he hit Hoyt. He wrote, "You will recall that several witnesses spoke of the fact that Thomson apparently ignored the yellow light and that could conceivably be the cause of his crash into Hoyt. If this is true, he should be penalized and fined."

Lamb asked Pritzbur, "Will you please talk with your men who witnessed his going past these lights and let me have your recommendations on it as Chief Steward of the race?"

It wasn't easy for anyone who knew the talented driver to question his judgment and ability. Pritzbur wrote back to Lamb on July 15 recounting that under strict interpretation of the rules, Thomson wasn't compelled to observe the caution until he crossed the starting line. Pritzbur recommended that no further action be taken. Lamb responded on July 20. "While in my mind there is no doubt that he did pass the caution lights, you are correct in the fact that a strict interpretation of the rule would require that he not actually be compelled to observe the yellow light until he crosses the starting line." He continued, "In other words, the yellow lights are put there for instantaneous warning of drivers of danger ahead and of course they have always been observed so far as we know. However, the actual signaling is controlled from the starting line—there can be no doubt about that."

Pritzbur held an important post. It was his job to officiate any race he was assigned. The AAA Contest Board relied on his official judgment. Lamb concluded his letter, "In view of these circumstances I suppose the best thing to do is to take your recommendation and do nothing about it, for the present at least. No doubt if nothing happens I will see you at the Grove this coming Sunday."

The controversy lingered on for years and still does in the minds of some. Pritzbur had made his recommendation, and Lamb made his decision. That should have ended it. The issue was resolved a long time ago. Langhorne was a difficult enough place to race at, boycotted by many of the Indianapolis 500 starters. It was a treacherous track that would eat up a car and its driver in a split second. Most believed the questioning of Thomson's judgment—that he committed a serious and dangerous violation of the rules—was necessary only because of complaints from unidentified witnesses, and not because it was observed by AAA Officials. Thomson was indeed a very aggressive racecar driver, but his record showed he used sound judgment. He was one of the most talented racecar drivers that ever raced in America.

Like so many others, Thomson kept going back to the "Big O." On June 24, 1956, he finished 18th. George Amick won that race. On June 2, 1957, driving the D. A. Lubricants Special, he won the event in record-setting fashion, covering the 100 miles in less than one hour and becoming the first driver to ever accomplish the feat at Langhorne. He averaged 100.174 miles per hour. On June 15, 1958, he finished 18th. In 1959 he crashed once again, this time during practice, and was unable to qualify. He went on to hold the 100-mile track records at Duquoin, Syracuse, New York, and Sacramento, California.

In 1953, for his first entry in the Indianapolis 500, Thomson started 33rd and finished 32nd, dropping out after only six laps with mechanical problems. In 1954 he started 4th and finished 24th, again having mechanical problems. He started 33rd and finished 4th in 1955, started 18th and finished 32nd in 1956, and started 11th and finished

12th in 1957. In 1958 he again had a rough time, dropping out after only 52 laps with mechanical problems. He had a very good race in 1959 at Indianapolis. He started on the pole and led for 40 of the 200 laps. But victory eluded him. He finished in third place. He came back in 1960 and ran a respectable race, starting 17th and finishing 5th. It looked like 1960 was going to be a good year. He was busy running a full USAC schedule in the Sprint car and Championship car divisions. By the time of the Allentown Fair, he had run some good finishes in addition to the fifth-place finish at Indianapolis. But there were no feature wins, and he went to the Allentown half-mile oval convinced he could win another fair sweepstakes.

The Allentown Fair had been good to him, and he showed his appreciation by driving one of Sam Traylor's first class Sprint cars to the win on September 21, 1957, and repeating in the same car on September 20, 1958. The best victories for Traylor, a local hotel owner and future member of the National Sprint Car Hall of Fame, were always the Allentown Fair wins.

For the September 24, 1960, event, Thomson was in a former Traylor car, later the Beal Offy and now the Stearly Motor Freight Offy, owned by Doug Stearly. He would be racing with USAC's best, including himself and Hinnershitz, who was now driving trucking magnate John Pfrommer's racecar, the former Nyquist Offy, a car with a bad reputation.

Also competing that day was a contingent of West Coast drivers who had launched an "invasion of the East." They campaigned in cars powered by Chevrolet V8 racing engines to compete against the Offenhauser powered cars. Among the invading drivers were young unknowns A.J. Foyt, Parnelli Jones, Jim Hurtubise, and Johnny White.

On the opening lap of the feature, Thomson was killed when he crashed through the inside fence on the backstretch.

If Hinnershitz was driving a car with a lurid past, then so was Thomson. The Stearly car was the same Beal Offy that Bill Schindler was killed in eight years earlier at virtually the same spot where Thomson died.

The next morning, the Sunday newspapers in Allentown, Reading, and elsewhere announced with large headlines that Jimmy Packard had won the tragic marred Allentown Fair feature event, that Johnny

Thomson had lost his life, and Hinnershitz announced that he would no longer drive racecars.

Packard's success was short-lived. He was killed in a USAC midget race the next weekend in Fairfield, Illinois.

Joie Chitwood

Passing the gas station in the *neighborhood* just east of Robesonia, Pennsylvania, on Route 422, halfway between Reading and Lebanon, practically everyone would notice the bright and fancy-painted cars sitting on trailers parked out back. The lettering on the side of each of them read "Joie Chitwood Thrill Show."

Texas-born George Rice "Joie" Chitwood was born on April 14, 1912, and eventually moved east to Pennsylvania under the sponsorship of Ralph Hankinson to be close to the auto-racing boom occurring on the East Coast. Later he became a successful businessman in the world of entertainment when he bought from Lucky Teeter's widow one of the most successful grandstand extra attractions in the history of state and county fairs. Teeter was killed on July 5, 1942, at the Indiana State Fair while performing the "Aerial Rocket Car Leap," a part of his thrill show.

Chitwood began driving race cars in Kansas in 1934 and was soon racing all over the country. He was a formidable competitor of Hinnershitz. Their high speed rivalry thrilled auto-racing fans.

In 1937, due to Chitwood's natural dark skin, Norm Witte, the CSRA secretary and PR man, titled Chitwood an "Indian." He created the name "Chief Wahoo" and applied it to Chitwood, who was running with CSRA at the time.

From that time forward, track announcers introduced Chitwood as Chief Wahoo, a full-blooded Cherokee Indian from Pawhuska, Oklahoma. Although Chitwood wasn't an "American Indian" and never lived in Oklahoma, his new nickname stuck. He became an "Indian" for the rest of his life.

In 1939 Chitwood won the first heat (12 laps) ever run at Williams Grove with a time of 6:10.20. He went on to win the 1939 AAA Eastern Sprint car championhip driving the O'Day Special.

He became car owner Hank O'Day's favorite driver. O'Day was

the owner of The Blackfront Tavern and Restaurant in Charleston, Illinois, a bar that featured illegal gambling, primarily slot machines. When the car wasn't being raced, O'Day displayed it in the Blackfront's vestibule. The Offenhauser-powered car was built in 1938 by California-based Indianapolis 500 racecar builder Louis "Curley" Wetteroth at a price tag of over $25,000. It was probably the most expensive Sprint car ever built up until that time. O'Day had the frame, running gear, and wire wheels chromed. The car became famous within racing circles before it ever entered a race. O'Day ran the car in AAA and CSRA competition throughout the Midwest and then brought it east to Pennsylvania. Chitwood set a new 10-mile world track record in the car at Savannah, Georgia, in 1938 and a new track record at Springfield, Illinois, in 1939. Others who drove the car were Pete Alberts, three-time Indianapolis 500 winner Mauri Rose, Johnny McDowell, and Hinnershitz, who flipped it.

In 1941 O'Day sold the car to Fred Peters who took it home to his thriving machine shop at Gasoline Alley in Paterson, and put Chitwood back in the car. In 1943 he sold the car to Texan Ben Musick. Between 1940 and 1950, Chitwood competed at Indianapolis, finishing fifth on three different occasions and becoming a member of the 100 Mile an Hour Club that was formed in 1935. To qualify for membership, a driver must have driven the full 500 miles at an average speed of at least 100 miles per hour without the aid of a relief driver. He was the first man ever to wear a seat belt while racing in the Indianapolis 500. Everyone in racing thought at the time that it was safer for a driver to be thrown from the car in the event of an accident. Chitwood didn't wear the seat belt for safety reasons, though; he wore it to minimize the bouncing around in the car that made it difficult for him to keep his foot on the accelerator.

Chitwood died January 3, 1988. He had briefly owned the garages and tavern at the famous Gasoline Alley in New Jersey until he sold them to Sam Nunis and later owned and operated a Chevrolet dealership in Zephyrhills, Florida. He had two sons, Joie Jr. and Tim. Joie Jr. had taken over the thrill show, and Joie Chitwood III became president of the Indianapolis Motor Speedway.

Bill Holland

Another member of the *neighborhood*, and a racing rival of Hinnershitz, was 1949 Indianapolis winner Bill Holland. Holland took up residence during the 1950s in the community of Wyomissing, on the western outskirts of Reading.

Born December 18, 1907 in North Carolina, Holland was raised in Philadelphia. He was named after his father Willard Holland, who was a major league shortstop. Before Holland began pursuing a career in auto-racing he tried out for the 1932 Olympic Games in ice-skating competition.

He began driving racecars in 1937; his first win came during the 1938 season in New York. He raced Sprint cars, mostly in Ralph Malamud's famous white and red Offy, and in 1940, he finished second in points behind AAA Eastern champion Chitwood. Holland went on to win the title in 1941. AAA combined the Championship and Sprint car points in 1946, which enabled Holland to have a very impressive year. He became national champion without ever driving a Championship car.

By 1947, however, he was a true contender in the Championship cars. After winning nine Sprint car races that year, winning at Milwaukee and Langhorne, he made his first start at Indianapolis finishing a surprising second to teammate Mauri Rose. Holland probably would have won if he hadn't been ordered to back off by the team boss.

He finished second to Rose again in 1948, won the race in 1949, and finished second in the rain-shortened 1950 race.

In November 1950, Holland was given a one-year suspension by AAA for competing in a non-AAA-sanctioned stock-car race. AAA suspended him despite Holland's overwhelming success at Indianapolis, placing second three times and winning the race once, all within a four-year period. He went to the media and expressed his anger, so AAA suspended him for another year. He did not go back to Indianapolis until 1953, when he qualified second but failed to finish the race. Holland retired from racing in 1959 and later moved with his wife Myra to Arizona, where they owned skating rinks in the Tucson area. Bill Holland died on May 20, 1984.

Buster Warke

Hinnershitz drove for *neighbor* Granville "Buster" Warke, who came from the town of Walnutport, just north of Allentown. Just as Hinnershitz was thrilled by the racers at the Reading Fairgrounds, Warke had a similar awakening at the Allentown Fair and other racetracks in the area. He wanted to be a racecar driver, but he was also drawn to the mechanics of the racecar.

After graduating from aviation school where he met driver Milt Marion, Warke got the opportunity to serve on Marion's pit crew. In the spring of 1935, in Charleston, West Virginia, Warke got the chance to drive. He didn't have a helmet, so he borrowed Hinnershitz's and they soon became close friends. They shared the helmet during qualifications, but Hinnershitz needed his helmet for the feature, so Warke was forced to use a cloth one. He finished fifth in the race that was won by Doc MacKenzie. Warke became an accomplished racecar driver, but his true talent was making a racecar go fast using the tools in his tool box.

Most of Warke's success as a driver was in the Midget ranks, but his true love was Sprint cars. In 1936 he purchased a car and put Frank McGurk in it, finding his own ride with other teams. He enjoyed a full career as a driver, mechanic, and car owner. When Williams Grove opened on May 21, 1939, Warke shared the front row with race winner Hinnershitz at the start of the first feature ever run on that half-mile track. After the war, Warke campaigned out west on the IMCA fair circuit driving Ben Shaw's airplane powered car.

When it was time to come back home, Warke signed on with car owner Ted Nyquist as a driver and mechanic. The other driver on the team was Joie Chitwood.

Throughout his career as a driver, Warke became a consistent threat to the competition, almost always running up front with the leaders. One of his best years was finishing fourth in the 1954 AAA Sprint car point standings behind Johnny Thomson, Hinnershitz, and Al Herman.

In 1956 Warke retired as a driver after a crash at the four-cornered half-mile track at Flemington. He had become a well-respected Offenhauser engine expert, so an immediate demand for his mechanical services emerged. Warke joined Fred Sclavi, a trucking-company owner from West Virginia, and their association took them all the way from the Championship car division to Indianapolis and Monza, Italy. Warke died on February 20, 2008, at the age of 93.

Ernie McCoy

Another *neighbor* was Ernie McCoy, born February 19, 1921, in Reading. He lived in the Gouglersville area, west of Reading, just a few miles from Hinnershitz's farm. Ernie's given name was Ernie Musser. He adopted the name McCoy when he began racing. McCoy competed in two Indianapolis 500s. One of the most underrated racecar drivers, this *neighbor* had a long and successful career in the Midget, Sprint car, and Championship car divisions. McCoy's driving career was born at the Yellow Jacket Speedway. As a teenager, McCoy was drawn to the racetrack after hearing about its thrilling, high-charged Midget racing. After hanging around for a while, he got a ride after telling a car owner he was an experienced driver who raced very successfully on the West Coast. He debuted there in 1941 and amazingly won feature races his first season. He went off to fight when Word War II broke out. Returning home after spending three years in the South Pacific as a Marine, McCoy teamed with car owner Stan Frankenfield from Ambler, Pennsylvania. They had a good working relationship that resulted in a very successful race team. After gaining a certain amount of fame and making a comfortable living racing, the good-looking McCoy was dubbed "lover boy" because of all the girls waiting for him at the pit gate.

He was a well-liked, personable man who was blessed with the friendship and camaraderie of his fellow drivers. On one occasion, a careless driver caused an accident that resulted in McCoy needing 500 stitches on the left side of his face. Veteran driver Len Duncan jumped from his racecar and forcefully pulled the errant driver out of the cockpit and nearly punched him. Then someone noticed that the seat belt was still closed in the offending driver's car.

McCoy started 20th in the 1953 Indianapolis 500 and finished 8th in the famous "Basement Bessie" car. Paul Russo and Ray Nichels had built the car in the basement of Russo's Indiana house during the winter of 1949-1950. Because of where it was built, the Russo-Nichels Special soon earned the moniker "Basement Bessie" while being raced in the AAA Championship division during the 1950 season. During its first run at Indianapolis, the car qualified in the seventh row and captured the imagination of race fans by running with the leaders for much of the race before the rain came at 345 miles. With Russo behind the wheel, Bessie finished ninth in the rain shortened 1950 Indianapolis 500. In 1951 Bessie was too slow to make the race, and in 1952 Russo didn't take the car to Indianapolis.

McCoy's rookie year was 1953, the same year for Bessie's second appearance in the race. Bessie was now under the ownership of the Stevens Racing Team, which competed at Indianapolis from 1950 until 1956. Andy Linden was the driver of the other Stevens car.

In the race won by Billy Vukovich, McCoy qualified the car 20th and finished 8th with an average speed of 123.404 miles per hour. Only the top eight cars finished the whole 200 laps, mostly due to the horrific weather conditions. It was dreadfully hot, with an air temperature of over 100 degrees; Carl Scarborough got out of his racecar, collapsed, and died of heat exhaustion. Finishing the race on the winning lap was a testament to the athletic McCoy's remarkable mental and physical stamina. He had been running fourth and probably would have finished in that position had he not been forced to make an unscheduled pit stop for tires.

In the next Championship car race, McCoy was in "Bessie" on the dirt at Milwaukee, finishing fifth behind winner Jack McGrath, Jimmy Bryan, Jerry Hoyt, and Bessie's builder and former owner Russo. There was a poor showing in June at Springfield; he dropped out after 20 laps. Rodger Ward took the Springfield win, and Hinnershitz finished 10th in Dr. Raymond Sabourin's car.

Then McCoy was involved in a strange deal at Detroit. On lap 73 of the Fourth of July 100-mile event, he flipped "Bessie," bringing out the red flag. The halt was so long that crewmembers started working on their cars, which was illegal under AAA rules. In another example of AAA logic, the race was reverted to lap 51, and McCoy was credited with sixth spot but was knocked out of the car due to injuries. Bob Scott took over "Bessie" for the "second half" of the race and brought her home ninth. Rodger Ward won the race on the one-mile dirt Michigan State Fairgrounds oval. On the first anniversary of the Michigan accident, McCoy was seriously injured in a Championship car race at Darlington, South Carolina, when the car crashed through the guard-rail and the front axle and wheels were torn off and hurled into the cockpit.

Next, McCoy got in the car for the tough Milwaukee 200, but he was too slow and missed the race. It was a long and busy year for McCoy. The car had become an aging "old lady." Bessie hung around for a few more years, playing out a long and interesting history that included a large cast of drivers.

In 1954 McCoy came back to Indianapolis and once again started 20th, finishing 16th in a Kurtis Kraft Offy. When the checkered flag was waved, Vukovich was once again in the winner's circle.

In the twi-light years of his career, McCoy concentrated on racing Midgets, a regular campaigner with ARDC, serving as a member of the Board of Directors of the organization. Later his sons Ernie and Barry Musser pursued successful, record-setting careers in drag racing. Like Chitwood, McCoy is a member of the Indianapolis Motor Speedway's exclusive and prestigious 100 Mile An Hour Club.

McCoy died February 4, 2001, in Port Orange, Florida.

Ottis Stine

Living on the western edge of the *neighborhood* in York, Pennsylvania, was Ottis Stine. He was born November 25, 1908, and died January 5, 2000, living to be 92 years of age. In 1934 Stine began a career that included driving Championship cars, Sprints cars, and Midgets. He made history in 1939 when he ran the first-ever hot lap at Williams Grove. As a rule, he stayed out of trouble, but on May 7, 1950, during the feature event at the Lakewood Park one-mile dirt track in Atlanta, Georgia, he rolled his very expensive $18,000 Offenhauser-powered Sprint car into the infield lake. The car became submerged in 30 feet of water. Luck wasn't with Pennsylvania drivers at Lakewood that year. Two months later on July 4, Hinnershitz went out over the bank and flipped after the right rear tire blew on lap three of his heat race. He suffered a fractured pelvis.

Stine never started in the Indianapolis 500, having failed in his

1952 attempt to qualify in the Scopa-Offenhauser. He did earn many AAA points, and when he retired in 1954, he held numerous track records. He won both AAA and URC Sprint car races. Stine stayed active in auto-racing until his death. He was a charter member of the York County Racing Club, founded in 1979, and was inducted into that organization's Hall of Fame in 1980.

Eddie Sachs

Neighbor Eddie Sachs enjoyed telling everyone he was the best racecar driver in the world, and in post-race interviews in victory circle, he proclaimed many times on the public address system that he knew he was going to win the race that day.

His egotistical harangue turned off some people. Others just laughed at the affable Sachs. Even though he might have carried things a bit far, most were quick to point out that Sachs earned a certain amount of bragging rights because he was, in fact, one of the best racecar drivers in the world. Sachs's rhetoric was all in jest. He was tagged "the Clown Prince of auto-racing" because of the publicity antics he pulled off throughout his career. Two of the many quotes attributed to him are: "If you can't win, be spectacular," and "Either win it, stack it, or blow it."

Sachs was born in Allentown on May 28, 1927. His parents were divorced and he was shuffled between Greensboro, North Carolina, where his father lived, and his grandmother who lived in Allentown. After graduating from military school, he enlisted in the Navy until he was discharged after narrowly escaping serious injury by a truck backing up to a loading dock.

In 1948 Sachs snuck into the pits at the Sprint car races at the Greensboro Fairgrounds and met Allentown's Dutch Culp. Sachs hung around the Culp pit all day, and it was probably at that time he decided to become a racecar driver. He dropped out of college and followed Culp from track to track, trying to make himself useful until he suddenly found himself back in Allentown broke and without any job prospects. He made it through winter and in the spring again began following the AAA Sprint car circuit until someone suggested he might increase his chances of getting a ride by hanging around the

AAA Class B circuit, where the less sophisticated cars and drivers competed.

Eventually Sachs did get a Sprint car ride at the Gratz, Pennsylvania Fairgrounds. He didn't do very well, making him more determined than ever to become a racecar driver. He talked owners into giving him rides on the Class B Midget circuit and eventually became a good enough driver to earn a ride in an Offenhauser-powered Midget.

In 1951 he started getting Sprint car rides, and he campaigned in the East, then late in the year migrated to the Midwest and eventually to the West Coast. With some luck, he earned a ride in a Championship car at Phoenix, Arizona, but crashed. In May at Indianapolis Sachs walked around without any pit credentials trying to find a ride. He got thrown out. Never discouraged, he worked on building a reputation by racing Sprint cars on the high banks of the Midwest while attempting to pass his Indianapolis rookie test in 1953, 1954, and 1955. Occasionally he'd earn a Championship car ride. In 1954 Sachs finished second in the AAA Midwest Sprint car standings, and at the same time started speaking out about poor safety conditions and low purses. He received what drivers who tried to stir things up got in the past—a suspension by AAA. He did what it took to get reinstated—he apologized. In 1955 he placed second again in points; the highlight that year was winning the 50-lap "Tommy Hinnershitz Day" feature event at Reading. Sachs had always been one of Hinnershitz's formidable rivals. They raced hard and fast against each other.

In 1956 Sachs finally passed his test at Indianapolis and qualified 34th—first alternate. Otherwise, 1956 turned out to be a good year; he won his first Championship car race at Lakewood Speedway.

In 1957 he started in the middle of the front row for his rookie run at Indianapolis. He finished 23rd after dropping out with mechanical problems. He got a dose of bad luck when he was seriously injured in a Midget accident at the 16th Street Speedway in Indianapolis and spent four months in the hospital.

Sachs experienced the best season of his career in 1958. He won the USAC Midwest Sprint car championship, finished fourth in the USAC Eastern Sprint car championship, and won two Championship car races at Langhorne Speedway and the Hoosier Hundred at the Indiana State Fairgrounds in Indianapolis. He led the Indianapolis 500 that year but was forced to drop out with mechanical problems and finished 22nd.

In 1959 Sachs again started in the middle of the front row but finished 17th after more mechanical problems. That year he won the Championship car race at Syracuse, finished second to Hinnershitz in the USAC Eastern Sprint car standings, and fourth in the Midwest standings. In 1960 he won the Championship car event at Trenton; Sachs finished 5th in the Eastern Sprint car chase and 10th in the Midwest.

In the 1960 and 1961 Indianapolis 500, Sachs started from the pole. He finished 22nd in 1960 after dropping out with magneto problems. In 1961 he had to pit for a new right-rear tire with just three laps to go. A. J. Foyt went on to beat Sachs by eight seconds. If he hadn't needed to make the tire change, Sachs probably would have won the 1961 Indianapolis 500. He was also runner-up in the 1961 Championship point standings. He scored wins in USAC stock car races on July 16 and August 17, 1961, at Milwaukee.

He finished 3rd at Indianapolis in 1962 and 17th in 1963 after crashing. Sachs was living in Detroit, Michigan, with his wife Nance and son Eddie Jr. when he was killed in the Indianapolis 500 on May 30, 1964. For years Sachs owned the Center Valley Inn and Motel in Center Valley, Pennsylvania, near Allentown. On occasions, when he decided to tend bar, the lucky patrons who happened to be there were treated to a superb entertainment event—a performance by Eddie Sachs.

Other than the obvious oval and road course difference between American and European racing, the cultural difference seems to be the "backyard garage" nature of racecar construction in America, so prevalent in the *neighborhood* in the *early years*, and certainly during the first 15-20 years after World War II. For example, Frank Kurtis, while building dozens of complete Midgets on the West Coast, also sold his Midgets in kit form. Kurtis-Kraft dealers like Frankie Del Roy at his Gasoline Alley speed shop sold components along with completely assembled Midget racecars. Men in small backyard shops could buy the components and weld together a first class Kurtis-Kraft Midget racecar.

In the Midwest, famous car builder A. J. Watson fabricated parts and even sold the blueprints to racecar teams and owners who wanted one of his revolutionary Indianapolis roadsters. Two classic examples of this method of racecar building was A. J. Foyt's 1961 Indianapolis winner, built by Ohioan Floyd Trevis, and the 1960-61 Dean Van Lines Indianapolis car built by Wayne Ewing and driven by Sachs. These cars shared such similar chassis designs that they were virtual clones of a Watson.

All the talented drivers and mechanics in the *neighborhood*, along with all the others across America, some prosperous and some just hanging on, kept their eyes focused on Tommy Hinnershitz, the most successful dirt track driver in America. In the *neighborhood*, he knew almost every one of them, and he met most others while traveling across the Midwest and up and down the East Coast. Whether on the racetrack as a driver or in the garage as a mechanic, they might not have been able to match Hinnershitz's talent, but they knew the closer they came to doing all the things he did, the better their own results could be.

Ernie McCoy poses in the Chapman Special at Indianapolis Motor Speedway with the car's pit crew in 1953.

L to R: Ray Harroun, 1911 Indianapolis winner, Pete DePaolo, 1925 winner, and Eddie Sachs, 1961 pole sitter, pose for a 1961 Firestone Tire publicity photo with the type of tire they each used while racing in the Indianapolis 500.

Armin Krueger/Greenfield Studio Photo

L to R: Red Riegel, Johnny Thomson, Tommy Hinnershitz, Ray Feinour, Floyd Delp, Bob Paulson, Russ Moyer, and Ernie McCoy, seated in a 3/4 Midget, gather at a Reading, Pennsylvania Traffic Club banquet circa 1958.

From the Delp Family collection

Sportswriter and screening committee member Gary Ludwig congratulates Tommy Hinnershitz during the Pennsylvania Sports Hall of Fame induction ceremony in 1975. At left is track announcer Steve Buch. In back is sports official Jim Beard. Pennsylvania Sports Hall of Fame Photo

Tommy Hinnershitz and car owner John Pfrommer celebrate a feature win at the Allentown, Pennsylvania Fair on September 26, 1959.

From the Carl Sweigart collection

The Holynski brothers from New York campaigned their revolutionary caged Sprint car with USAC (the United States Auto Club). The racecar is pictured here in 1964.

From the Holynski Family collection

Jim Hurtibuise #96 takes the caged Holynski Engineering Special into the 1st turn circa 1965.

From the Holynski Family collection

A. J. Foyt in 1964

Armin Krueger/Greenfield Studio Photo

Mario Andretti in 1965

Armin Krueger/Greenfield Studio Photo

Red Riegel at Terre Haute, Indiana, in 1965

From the Riegel Family collection

Chuck Engel #93 and Jud Larson #4 during Sprint car action in 1964

Armin Krueger/Greenfield Studio Photo

Don Branson in 1965

Armin Krueger/Greenfield Studio Photo

Tommy Hinnershitz comes off the 4th turn during his time trial at Terre Haute, Indiana, in 1958.

From the Carl Sweigart collection

Rivals Jan Opperman #99 and Kenny Weld #29 battle it out in Super Sprint cars fitted with cages and wings popularized in the 1970s.

Gary Ludwig Photo

Red Riegel in 1965. Car owner Louis Seymour is pictured in back.

From the Riegel Family collection.

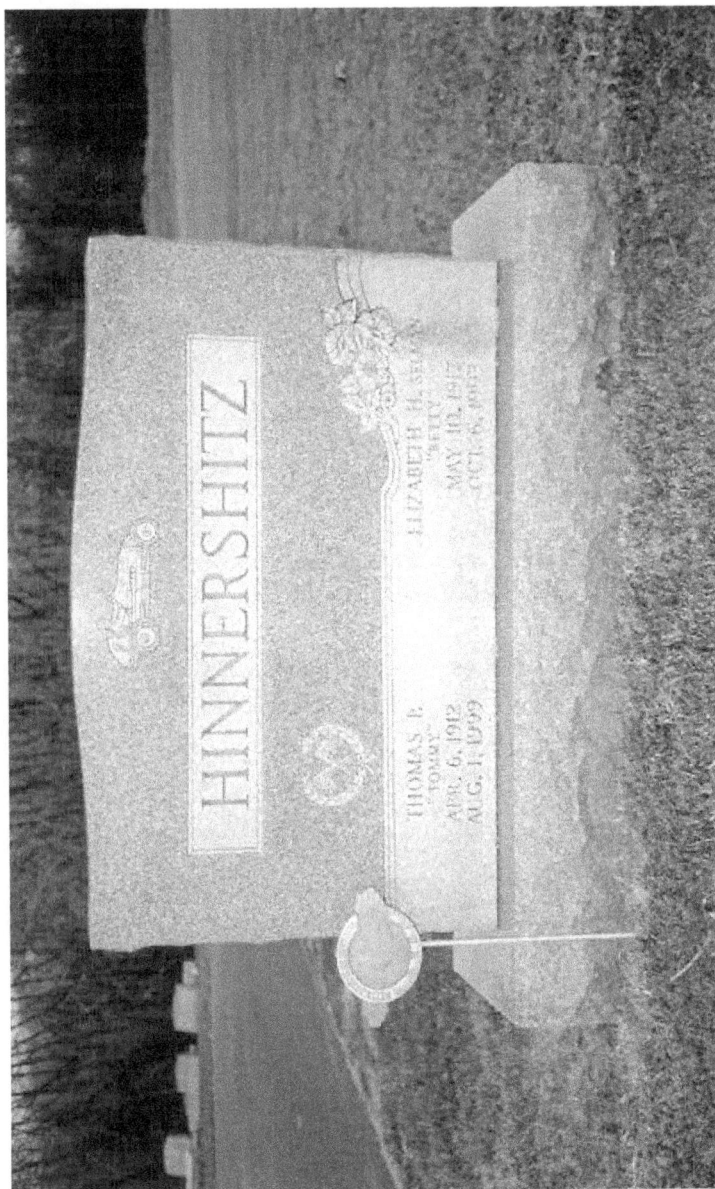

FINAL RESTING PLACE
Spies's Church Cemetery, Alsace Township, Berks County, Pennsylvania
TOMMY HINNERSHITZ: April 6, 1912 – August 1, 1999 • BETTY HINNERSHITZ: May 10, 1917 – October 6, 1993

Gary Ludwig Photo

Chapter 6

The War Ends

When World War II broke out, auto-racing in America stopped. Tommy Hinnershitz raced an abbreviated schedule in 1942 that ended in July. He didn't compete again until September 1945. Like thousands of other young men, he was inducted into the United States Army. Then he was discharged because of medical reasons related to his back. All he could do was wait until the bloody fighting ended and the high-speed wars on the dirt tracks resumed.

Many of Hinnershitz's rivals who had served in battle compared the infamous Langhorne Speedway with the battlefields of Europe or the Pacific Islands. Mike Nazurak, who served as a Marine during the war, had said more than once how he survived the hell of Guadalcanal but wasn't sure he would survive Langhorne. He didn't; he was killed there May 1, 1955, in Ted Nyquist's Sprint car, the Nyquist Offy. Nazurak was called "Iron Mike." He raced Midget cars, Sprint cars, and Championship cars. Eventually he won the track championships at Staten Island and Rhinebeck, New York, in 1947 and won over 20 feature races at Middletown, New York, winning that track's 1948 point crown. The following year, Nazurak won the 1949 ARDC Midget car championship. Nazaruk joined AAA in 1950, competing in that organization's Sprint car and Midget divisions. He finished second in the 1951 Indianapolis 500 and competed at Indianapolis two more times, finishing 21st in 1953 and 5th in 1954.

Since 1939 Hinnershitz had been campaigning as a member of Ted Horn's racing team. Practically every driver that competed against Horn admired and respected him. There were drivers, mechanics, car owners, officials, and fans who all said that Horn's accomplishments on the track would never be matched. Hinnershitz agreed.

While the Championship division title always seemed to be up for grabs, however there would soon be a driver who overpowered and dominated the competition in the Sprint car division. With the end to the fighting overseas, things slowly got back to normal in the auto-racing world, and when the 1947 season got underway, Hinnershitz began playing a dual role. When Horn decided to cut back on the size of his team, Hinnershitz bought the Horn car that was built primarily to run on high-banked tracks. Horn had raced it on the Midwest high-banked ovals like Salem and Winchester, Indiana, and Dayton, Ohio.

Now that he was his own boss, Hinnershitz prepared himself and his own racecar, now painted powder blue and christened "Bluebird", to become a successful winning combination. All of his cars became "Bluebirds" until he adopted the now famous yellow, blue, and red colors of his sponsor Miracle Power Products. While towing "Bluebird" to the first few racetracks, Hinnershitz was cautiously optimistic about his chances for success.

Chapter 7

Westward Ho'!

Hinnershitz had always done well racing in the Midwest. But few people realize that he ventured much further west than Indiana back in 1937. The Hoosier state had been good to him. There in the Indianapolis 500, he joined an exclusive club of daring *champions.* To most racecar drivers, competing at Indianapolis is the ultimate professional accomplishment. Here the best get to compete against each other on a higher plain. Hinnershitz established himself as the best on the dirt tracks, but his starts and finishes at Indianapolis bring a special respect from the casual observer of the sport.

On August 17, 1958, Hinnershitz won the famous and much publicized East versus West USAC Sprint Car race at Terre Haute, Indiana. He beat drivers half his age in the Hiram Hillegass-built John Pfrommer Offy, formerly the Nyquist Offy. There weren't going to be any more Hillegass cars. The last one was built in 1957, and famed Illinois-based car owner Ralph Helm bought it.

Being back in Indiana for the special Terre Haute race was a fitting way for Hinnershitz to finish up his final campaign far from home. The half-mile clay oval track, built in 1952, is part of the Wabash Valley Fairgrounds and is truly a racetrack of champions. The day of the race was steeped with tradition and showmanship. Following the script of so many AAA sanctioned events, and now picked-up by USAC, the sparkling, brightly painted racecars sat on the front stretch during intermission. Fans could walk up to the fence and gawk at the expensive cars with their chromed header pipes, radius rods, bumpers, and now the latest accessory—the chromed roll bar. Occasionally a driver would walk over to the fence and sign autographs; it was a relaxing, pleasant pause before the finale's intensity put everyone on the edge of their seat. It was all the stuff that made America fall in love with athletes. The slower pace also allowed the drivers and car owners to bask in the glory. And just as the first pitch at a baseball game gets everyone excited in a slower and gentler fashion, the drop of the green flag creates loud and immediate frenzy.

The feature race Hinnershitz won that day turned out to be his 100th AAA/USAC victory. Nobody knows how many others he won. The actual number has been lost in the myths of the eras through which he traveled. The recorded career statistics are certainly fallible. Race promoters who worked out of a duffel bag kept no records. The memories of the early rowdies who did the wrench work, and the ones who had the courage to do the dare deviling, never suspected anybody would ever care who won, who crashed, or even who died. Those victories are lost forever. Even the faint memories of some of them have gone to the graves with those who won them.

After the feature event that day, the 100th win by a living legend, the fans stayed to witness the honoring by the track and the Hoosier Auto-racing Fan Club. Hinnershitz thanked everyone for keeping a record of his wins. He had not realized he just won his 100th feature race.

Seeking fame and fortune

Hinnershitz first went west in search of feature wins in 1937. He jumped back and forth between east and west, running the Midwestern and Western tracks while at the same time maintaining his schedule in the East. On July 11, 1937, driving the Sex Perriman-owned Sprint car on the half-mile dirt track at Frontier Park in Cedar Rapids, Iowa, Hinnershitz finished third in his heat but failed to place in the 30-lap feature. Frontier Park, in existence since 1925, was later named Cedar Rapids Speedway, and today is known as Hawkeye Downs Speedway. Later the track was paved. Over the years the speedway has hosted USAC Sprint cars, Midgets, the IMCA Summer Series, and various other stock car and open-wheel racing series.

A week later, on July 18 in Chicago at the Cook County Fairground's half-mile dirt track, Hinnershitz brought the Perriman-owned car home third in the 50-lap feature. That track was located at North Avenue and River Road and featured auto-racing in the 1930s until 1940. Chicago's fair board, organized in the 1870s, had sought a permanent location for a half-mile track for harness racing and speed trials. Horse racing was so popular that by 1900, 80 of the 102 Illinois county fairs featured trotting and pacing competitions. Soon, bicycle races, balloon rides, and eventually auto-racing, airplane demonstrations, and fireworks were regular attractions.

After this good feature finish, Hinnershitz went home for scheduled races in the East, not to go back to the West until late summer. On August 22, 1937, Hinnershitz and the Perriman racing team showed up at Milwaukee, Wisconsin, to race on the one-mile dirt track. He finished third in his 10-mile heat but failed to place in the 25-mile feature. The Milwaukee track had its beginning around 1876 as a private horse-racing track. In 1891 the track was purchased by the State of Wisconsin for a permanent site for the Wisconsin State Fair. The first auto race was run on September 11, 1903. William Jones of Chicago won a five-lap speed contest, setting the first track record with a 72-second, 50-miles-per-hour lap. Barney Oldfield set the track record in 1905 and raised his speed in 1910 to 70.159 miles per hour. In 1911 Ralph DePalma won the first Milwaukee championship car race a week before his Indianapolis 500 win, and in 1915, Louis Disbrow won the first 100-mile event, averaging 62.5 miles per hour.

It was at Milwaukee in 1917 that Oldfield tested the "Golden Submarine," the gold colored car that completely enclosed the driver. Oldfield beat DePalma in a series of 10 to 25-mile match races.

The first Championship car event was rained out on July 17, 1933. Wilbur Shaw and the other drivers convinced the track promoters to run the race the following day, and the "Rain Date" was born.

The 1937 Championship car event was best known for running 96 laps instead of the scheduled 100 due to a scoring error. That race was won by Rex Mays. Ten years later, the tradition of hosting the "race after the Indianapolis 500" began. On August 26th, 1937, Hinnershitz and Perriman were back at Milwaukee but didn't start because of mechanical problems. Bad luck continued on September 19 when the team went back to the Cook County Fairgrounds. Mechanical problems prevented Hinnershitz from starting.

Next on Hinnershitz's agenda was some Midget racing. As a result of their heightened popularity, Hinnershitz competed in a lot of Midget races during the years 1937-39, in addition to racing Sprint cars. On November 17, 1937, he appeared at the Will Rogers Coliseum in Ft. Worth, Texas, on the 1/8-mile dirt oval inside that colossal building. He finished fifth in his 10-lap heat and fifth again in the 25-lap feature.

The Coliseum, part of a complex that includes an auditorium, exhibit halls, an equestrian center, and nine livestock areas, was completed in 1936, the year of the Texas Centennial, and is the first domed structure of its kind in the world. It was named for Will Rogers, the well-known American humorist, who was born in 1879 and died in an airplane crash in 1935. Rogers was a very close friend of Amon G. Carter, who is remembered in Fort Worth as a dynamic business and civic leader.

Four days later, on November 21, 1937, Hinnershitz competed in more Midget competition on the 1/5-mile track at the Houston Speedway, in Houston, Texas, finishing ninth in the 25-lap feature. Two drivers who Hinnershitz raced against there were Bill Schindler, a man he would meet up with again, and Carl Forberg. Forberg started racing midgets in the Omaha, Nebraska, area in 1935 and then moved to Detroit, and raced Midgets with the AAA. He raced in the Indianapolis 500 in 1951, but injuries cut his career as a driver short. In the 1960s and 1970s, Forberg became a famed car owner of first class equipment, fielding a USAC Sprint car driven by Johnny Parsons, Jr., Ralph Ligouri, and Todd Gibson.

It was reported that the first Midget race ever to run in the state of Texas was at Houston Speedway on October 31, 1937. More than 9,000 people jammed into its 7,000 seats. It was definitely a golden time for Midget racecar competition. Houston Speedway and the track in San Antonio were paying 50 percent of the ticket sales with a $500 guarantee, the same purse that Freeport Speedway on Long Island, New York, was paying. Eventually Houston Speedway offered a $750 guarantee. The speedway suspected the response by racing teams would be so overwhelming that they advertised the field of drivers was limited and it was necessary to write or wire for an OK before arriving. It was announced that the program would follow the Freeport Speedway guideline, consisting of four 8-lap heats, two 10-lap semi-features, a 12-lap consolation, and a 20-lap feature.

The Houston Speedway was filling the stands with twice-a-week races. Inevitably, the cold weather came. It was earlier and colder than normal, the worst in 20 years. Some drivers planned to go east and race on the indoor tracks. Hinnershitz would end his season with two more races at Houston after a sixth place finish in the 25-lap feature at the Will Rogers Coliseum on November 24, 1937. On November 25 at Houston, he finished third in his 10-lap heat, sixth in the 12-lap semi-feature, and fourth in the 15-lap consolation. On November 26, 1937, he finished third in his 10-lap heat and seventh in the 25-lap feature.

It was time to go home. Hinnershitz's first venture west was a learning experience. As his young career developed, it was logical for the Eastern-based driver to race closer to home, especially with the abundance of racetracks in the East racing Sprint cars.

Throughout the 1930s and just before and after World War II, Hinnershitz did return to campaign at many of those Western tracks and soon added Springfield, Illinois, Soldier's Field in Chicago, and Columbus, Ohio, to the schedule, along with tracks in Arizona, Nevada, and Oklahoma, as well as southern tracks in North Carolina, Georgia, Florida, Louisiana, and Alabama.

Self-employment on the high banks

Hinnershitz was for the first time a car owner after buying one of the Horn cars during the winter of 1946. The rail-frame car was built by Red and Russ Garnant and sold to Horn in 1941 to run specifically on high-banked tracks, so it was logical to tow it out west where the high-banked tracks were. Hinnershitz's first stop was the half-mile, high-banked dirt track in the hills of Southern Indiana at Salem. On June 22, 1947, he repeated what he did at Williams Grove in 1939—he won the new track's first ever feature, a 20-lap main event. He came back on July 4 and did it again. Salem Speedway turned out to be fertile ground for the newly self-employed driver. The car performed beautifully on banked turns; however, because of the car's longer wheelbase, it wasn't suited for the half-mile dirt ovals back east. Hinnershitz hired car builder Bob Blake to put together a shorter wheelbase car to run on the flat half-mile tracks.

More than 50 years later, Salem Speedway plays host to USAC and other sanctioning organizations. Since Hinnershitz baptized the oval on that sunny June day in front of over 7,000 fans, many of the biggest names in racing have competed there. Great drivers like Ted Horn, Parnelli Jones, A. J. Foyt, Mario Andretti, and Bobby and Al Unser have won features at Salem. Originally known for its treacherous and intimating dirt high banks, it was paved after a few seasons. Through the years, it's often been said by many, "If a man goes fast at Salem, he can go fast anywhere."

Thus far, Hinnershitz was doing very well on the high banks. Later in the season, he towed to Winchester Speedway, located approximately 90 miles east of Indianapolis. On August 10, 1947, he finished second in the 20-lap feature. The speedway is the oldest half-mile track in America built specifically for auto-racing and is also known as the "World's fastest half-mile." Its 37-degree banking, one of the steepest in auto-racing, enables drivers to run very fast speeds. The track, built in a cornfield by Frank Funk, opened in 1916. It operated as a half-mile flat, oiled dirt oval until 1921, then as a half-mile high-banked dirt oval from 1922 until 1929. From 1929 through 1942 and after World War II from 1945 through 1951, the surface was once again oiled to harden it and keep down the dust. The track was paved in 1951. Funk promoted the track from 1914 through 1963. Through the years, many of the best racecar drivers competed there, primarily in AAA and USAC Sprint cars.

The next stop on Hinnershitz's first time high-bank racing tour was the half-mile Dayton Speedway on the outskirts of Dayton in southwest Ohio. On September 7, 1947, Hinnershitz won his 10-lap heat and finished second in the 20-lap feature on the paved track, proving that the dirt-tracker could also go fast on pavement.

The track opened as a 5/8-mile flat square dirt oval in 1934. In 1937 Funk, purchased the Dayton track and in 1939 converted it into a high-banked half-mile dirt oval. After closing the track in 1943 and 1944 because of World War II, Funk reopened it in September 1945 after raising the banking and putting oil on the surface. In the fall of 1946, he paved the track. Dayton Speedway closed in 1982. Today Dayton Speedway is a landfill.

Chapter 8

Racing in the Backyard

Hinnershitz proved he could run fast on the dirt and paved high-banked half-mile tracks, the big one-mile ovals at the gigantic Midwest state fairs, the cramped stadium Midget tracks, both indoor and outdoor, and eventually on the bricks at Indianapolis. He was versatile, competitive, and proficient wherever he ran, regardless of the surface or the layout.

Because he was brought up an Eastern dirt track driver, naturally he was most prolific on the flat half-mile horse tracks; just about every fairground in the Eastern United States had one. It was on these tracks, and a few Eastern one-mile ovals, that Hinnershitz would race most of the time, and he sought to master them one by one. They were in his backyard—it didn't take a lot of travel time to get there. They were the tracks where big time promoter Ralph Hankinson and assorted small time promoters did their business. Year after year, the fans flocked to the ticket windows with thousands of entertainment dollars.

What makes an athlete good is the desire to be the best at every outing. Hinnershitz sought victory every time he raced, always pushing to get to the checkered flag first. It was at the Reading Fairgrounds that a young boy named Thomas Paul Hinnershitz was first exposed to automobile racing. He raced there, crashed there, and eventually won there. He called it his home track; it was where his fans knew him best and loved him the most.

The Reading dirt oval was the closest any half-mile racetrack could be to perfect. The flat turns were long and sweeping, the straight-aways wide. The surface was always good even before it got its clay surface. The track rarely broke up; there were no holes and ruts. Track preparation by the Reading Fairgrounds was a top priority even in the days before Lindy Vicari took over as promoter. Vicari was a master at track preparation who personally supervised every aspect of the job and then operated the grader himself to do the final touches before race time, creating a smooth textured surface with multi-grooves in the turns. The track opened on September 20, 1924 and operated until May 17, 1942. Grady Garner won the opening day feature. The track reopened after World War II on May 26, 1946 and operated until June 29, 1979. The track even held drag racing on the front stretch during the 1960s.

Vicari, while continuing to schedule Sprint car racing, brought weekly stock car racing to the track in the early 1950s. These cars started out as stripped down and gutted flathead-powered old coupes and coaches, eventually evolving into the famous and powerful Reading-style modified stock cars.

In the early 1970s, a group of businessmen decided to build a one-mile thoroughbred horse-racing complex in the heart of Central Pennsylvania. Vicari got involved and supervised the construction of a half-mile clone of the Reading track next to the one-mile horse track. Penn National Speedway opened in 1971, and the horse track opened the following year. The speedway closed in 1997 and was demolished in 2006.

Another favorite stop for Hinnershitz was Williams Grove, probably the best-known half-mile oval in America. The speedway is located south of Harrisburg, Pennsylvania just, off Route 15 in Monroe Township, Cumberland County.

Around 1850, the Williams family began hosting picnics on a wooded section of their farm that bordered a creek. The picnic area became popular among their neighbors, and soon people began building cottages for summer visits. Later a Merry-Go-Round was installed for the children. After the Grangers held a successful fair there in 1872, the picnic grounds were developed into fairgrounds. By 1887 there was an auditorium, campground, summer cottages, exhibition halls, and a hotel.

The Richwine family bought the park in 1924, and Roy Richwine turned the fairgrounds into an amusement park. In 1937 master promoter Ralph Hankinson helped design and lay out a track for auto-racing next to the park, and Richwine began building Williams Grove Speedway. Then Hankinson and Richwine made their pact; they would not run against each other.

The track opened on May 21, 1939. Joie Chitwood won the first heat, and Hinnershitz won the first feature race ever run there; his time for the 40-lap feature was 19:26.33. He would go on to win a total of 19 features there. Over the years, Roy Richwine, followed by his son Robert, ran the speedway successfully, making periodic improvements. The covered wooden grandstand was replaced with spacious bleachers, the worn out and famous pagoda-style official's stand in the infield was demolished, and the first and second turns were rebuilt and made higher and wider with a slight banking and a walkway tunnel underneath. New modern offices were built on the outside of turn one. There is a walkway bridge over the backstretch.

Because of its half-mile length, grandstands and convenient location, Williams Grove quickly became the premier racetrack in the area. Neighboring tracks suffered attendance loss as some of the best racers began competing at Williams Grove. The track presented local modified stock car racing and AAA, USAC, and URC sanctioned Sprint car racing and occasionally the Championship cars. The ARDC Midgets also have been featured over the years, and NASCAR late-model stock cars drew enormous crowds. Robert Richwine sold the park and speedway in 1971.

Ho-Ho-Kus Speedway was located in the town of Ho-Ho-Kus, New Jersey. The half-mile dirt track, built in 1906 as a horseracing track, featured auto-racing from 1912 until July 4, 1938, when the town council banned all auto-racing after Henry Guerand and Vince Brehm were involved in a tragic accident. Guerand's racecar exited the track and hit a car in the parking lot, killing two spectators, including a 10-year-old boy. The accident wasn't the first tragedy at the track. On May 31, 1934, 23-year-old driver George Herzog was killed when his car flipped three times. Famed thrill show owner Jack Kochman had promoted the speedway, drawing first- class, nationally known drivers.

Hinnershitz raced at Hohokus 15 times beginning in 1934. His first win came on June 28, 1936, when he captured the 30-lap feature. He won again on October 18, again winning the 30-lap feature. He made his last start at Hohokus on May 29, 1938. The track fell into disrepair and was sold in 1950 to make way for a housing development.

After the war Kochman, with 10 cars and 4 drivers, began his thrill show, booked at many of the state and county fairs formerly played by Lucky Teeter before he was killed. He acquired a motorcycle track circuit in the Eastern United States and attracted 50,000 fans to the Langhorne Speedway in Philadelphia for 100-mile Midget auto races. Kochman also promoted indoor Midget racing during the winter at the Kingsbridge Armory in New York City. But perhaps his greatest pre-war racing promotion success took place at the 1/7-mile high-banked board track in the Nutley Velodrome in New Jersey, which was the only banked board oval in the world.

Hinnershitz competed in the first auto race ever run at the Velodrome, won by Paul Russo, on April 3, 1938. Hinnershitz finished fourth in the 35-lap feature. He appeared a total of 41 times there. Even though he usually finished with the frontrunners, he only won once at the treacherous track. Some critics described the racing at the Velodrome as madness. It was a dangerous place to race because of the lethal combination of extremely tight racing conditions and the high speeds attained by the cars.

Three drivers were killed in 60 races before racing stopped at the Velodrome on August 26, 1939. Hinnershitz got upside down on September 28, 1938, and was involved in a spectacular accident on April 2, 1939, when he was thrown from the car. The small, 45-degree banked wood oval was built for bicycle racing in 1933 and was also the site of four boxing matches. When interest in bicycle racing waned, the track was closed in 1937.

Kochman re-opened the track for Midget auto-racing and ran it until it was finally shut down after 24-year-old California driver

Karl Hattel was killed when his racecar crashed into the guardrail. This was the third fatal accident in less than one year. New Jersey native Charlie Heliker was the first driver to lose his life. He burned to death on October 9, 1938. The town council of Nutley, branding the track as "homicidal," revoked the Velodrome's license to race after each of the previous two fatalities, but the State Supreme Court overturned the revocations each time.

On April 3, 1939, over 6500 fans watched as 26-year-old Guerand of Irvington, New Jersey, was killed instantly when his car, speeding 65 miles an hour, crashed into a guardrail. He was decapitated by one of the heavy cables. Bill Schindler, the one-legged driver from nearby Freeport, Long Island, suffered a deep cut under the eye when his car brushed Guerand's. The Velodrome was demolished in February 1942.

Auto-racing came to the New York State Fair at the very beginning of the 20th century, when such renowned names as Barney Oldfield, Wilbur Shaw, and Ralph DePalma came to thrill the fairgoers. Through the years, the AAA and later the USAC Championship cars were a regular attraction on the one-mile flat dirt track.

Hinnershitz first raced there on September 10, 1938, but was forced out with mechanical problems on lap 67 of the 100-lap event. He raced there a total of six times; his best finish was third in the 100-mile race on September 2, 1940, in John Gerber's car behind second place finisher George Robson and race winner Rex Mays.

The race programs at Syracuse usually went pretty smoothly, but there were exceptions. At the September 10, 1949, race, a dispute over prize money delayed the start of the race for more than an hour, and the fans were becoming more and more restless. Mays prevented what might have developed into a major riot when, without speaking a word, he got into his car and started circling the track. One by one of the other drivers followed. Hinnershitz finished 10th that day. At that time, Mays was one of the most respected drivers in auto-racing.

Like most other speedways, Syracuse endured tragic racing accidents that resulted in the loss of life. Some tracks have tragedies that become catastrophes in their history. Syracuse is one of those tracks.

On September 17, 1911, nine people were killed and fourteen others seriously injured as the result of one of the worst accidents in the history of automobile racing in this country. The accident occurred when a tire blew out on the racecar driven by Lee Oldfield (no relation to Barney Oldfield), and he crashed through the guardrail into the crowd—jammed together eight to ten deep—on the 43rd lap of the scheduled 50-lap race.

Six people were killed instantly, two others died on the way to the hospital, and another died at the hospital. Oldfield was taken to the hospital with a fractured rib and severe internal injuries. Immediately, the rough track conditions were blamed by the other drivers for the blown tire that caused Oldfield to lose control of the car.

President William Howard Taft, who was a guest at the fair, had departed only a few minutes before the accident occurred. The track had been watered to keep down the dust when the presidential vehicles departed.

Prominent drivers DePalma and Bob Burman both refused to race in the previous event on the program because of the track's conditions. This delayed the start of the 50-mile event, and the crowd grew by a few thousand because of the delay. DePalma, who had come to America at age 10 with his Italian immigrant parents, had raced in 111 events up until this Syracuse event and had become famous because he had won 74 of them.

Early in the race, DePalma, who was leading, developed tire troubles, and the fan's excitement increased as Oldfield began gaining ground on him. Then Oldfield's right front tire started losing its tread, and it could be seen flapping while he completed each lap without slowing down. The officials were urging him to come in for a tire change, but his mechanic was signaling him instead to increase his speed. Oldfield decided to increase his speed at the expense of caution and wait to stop when DePalma would also need to stop. Then as Oldfield got up right behind DePalma, the tire blew and he lost control, crashing the car into the crowd and traveling 20 feet before it stopped.

Startled by the explosion of Oldfield's tire and his car leaving the track, DePalma was nevertheless unaware that the accident had been so serious, so he kept racing. Though the officials were aware people were injured and killed, they refused to end the race, and De-Palma finished the 50 laps. Almost immediately after crossing the finish line, one of DePalma's rear tires blew.

There was much criticism of Oldfield at the races the following month at Fairmount Park in Philadelphia. Despite the opinion of the local government officials in Syracuse and AAA that he wasn't at fault, many people considered him reckless and responsible for the vast death and injury.

Others searched for peculiar reasons why the car left the track. These explorations helped start one of the superstitions that became part of auto-racing folklore—Oldfield was driving a green racecar.

Langhorne Speedway, located in the Philadelphia suburbs, was built on a swamp by a group of Philadelphia businessmen who held their first race on June 12, 1926. Freddie Winnai of Philadelphia won the 50-lap main event. From the beginning, the track's unique circular configuration earned it the "Big O" nickname, along with another–the "Big Left Turn." The business group operated the track through the 1929 season, staging races, some as long as 100 laps, on holidays. The track was not financially successful, due mostly to poor management and bad track conditions that kept crowds sparse.

The well-established promoter Hankinson and Lucky Teeter took over the speedway in 1930. They brought in the AAA Championship cars for 100-lap races and shorter distance events for Sprint cars. AAA sanctioned Championship cars raced at the track 12 times between 1930 and 1955. USAC sanctioned the Championship cars there from 1956 to 1970. One of the first stock car races in the Northeast was held at Langhorne in 1940. Roy Hall of Atlanta, Georgia, won the 200-lap event. The AMA (American Motorcycle Association) sanctioned championship Motorcycle races there between 1935 and 1956. When Hankinson and Teeter both died during World War II, John Babcock and his family took over as promoters until 1951.

The track became known as one of the more dangerous speedways in auto-racing. Famed drivers lost their lives or were seriously injured there. Many of the accidents were spectacular, mostly because of rough track conditions and the high speeds.

Irv Fried and Al Gerber took over Langhorne from Babcock in 1951. In 1965 the co-promoters paved the track and re-worked the track layout into a "D" shape by building a straightaway across the back stretch. The land increased in value and became a desirable piece of commercial real estate. Fried and Gerber sold the property to mall developers in 1967. After the sale, the track operated for five more years.

Hinnershitz made his first appearance at Langhorne on August 11, 1934. He never won there. His best finishes were a second in the Sprint car 50-lap feature on May 14, 1939, and fifth in the 100-lap Championship car race on October 16, 1949.

In 1964, car-owner Doug Stearly, who owned the Sprint car Johnny Thomson was killed in, recommended Mario Andretti for a ride in Lee Glessner's racecar for the Langhorne race on June 21. Hinnershitz was serving as Glessner's chief mechanic. It was Andretti's first time driving in the Championship car division. Unlike most of the front-runners, Glessner's car lacked power steering. Roaring into Langhorne's notorious "Puke Hollow" in a racecar with power steering was difficult enough, but without it could be hard work, especially when running a 100-lap race. "Puke Hollow," located between the first and second turns, crept up on a driver after passing the starter's stand and was one of the most dangerous sections of the racetrack, killing quite a few drivers, including the great Jimmy Bryan in 1960. The water table was a little higher there and as a result, the racecars dug grooves a little deeper into that softer section of the moist track. Then the sun baked the grooves into unforgiving ruts that caused the racecars to bounce while the drivers tried to keep set up and on the throttle for the almost constant 100-miles-per-hour power slides.

Over the years Andretti has said he was lucky to have Hinnershitz with him that day. Hinnershitz watched the young driver during warm-ups and then gave him advice how to run the track, especially when to back off going into the turns during time trials. Andretti qualified eighth and hung on to finish ninth in the race. The final race at Langhorne Speedway was on October 17, 1971, for modified stock cars.

On August 16, 1937, during his Midget-racing era, Hinnershitz appeared in his first race at Yellow Jacket Speedway. He finished second in his heat but spun out in the 20-lap feature. It didn't take him long to figure out the fastest way around the small track. The following week, on August 23, he won the 30-lap feature.

Hinnershitz went on to race 20 times at the track and won two more times. A highlight of his Yellow Jacket appearances was finishing fourth in the 150-lap Atlantic States Championship event for Midgets on October 4, 1938. On July 10, 1939, he brought out the red flag when he flipped after hitting the fence on the 31st lap of the 40-lap feature.

The track opened on May 24, 1938, with Wally Sechrist as the promoter. He ran Midget races on Tuesday and Friday nights. In 1940 he paved the track and switched from AAA to ARDC sanctioning. After World War II, racing resumed, but in 1949 the track started to phase out the Midgets in favor of Stock cars. In 1951 a new Yellow Jacket Speedway was built in the front portion of Langhorne Speedway's infield.

Hinnershitz made his first start at the Flemington, New Jersey Fair Speedway on September 1, 1934. He won the consolation but didn't place in the feature. He made 18 starts at the track, winning his first feature on September 3, 1938. He won a total of four times at the track. His close friend Parke Culp was killed there on September 7, 1936. Hinnershitz's last race at Flemington was September 5, 1955.

Flemington Speedway opened in 1915 as a square half-mile dirt track with four corners. In 1917 the grandstand was built. The track was enlarged to a 5/8-mile semi-banked D-shaped dirt oval in 1966. The track continuously lost money after it was paved at the end of the 1990 season and closed on November 8th, 2002, after the owners decided the Flemington Fair was no longer profitable. The grandstand was knocked down in January 2006, and the speedway and fair buildings were demolished in 2007 to make way for a planned shopping center. Before it closed, Flemington was America's oldest weekly running speedway. A heavily rural farming area surrounded the small town of Flemington for many years. The 2000 census listed Flemington's population as 4,201 people. The town was the location of the Lindbergh kidnapping trial in its Hunterdon County courthouse. On February 13, 1935, a jury found Bruno Richard Hauptmann guilty of the kidnapping and murder of Charles Lindbergh's infant son.

The first auto race ever held at the Allentown Fairgrounds was on July 31, 1915. Like virtually all the county fair racetracks in Pennsylvania, it was a half-mile dirt horse track. Allentown's track was laid out in 1888. In 1911 the fair board built a grandstand.

Joe Lambert was the first auto race victor at the Allentown track. The great success of auto-racing at Allentown can be attributed to the hugely successful Allentown Fair drawing thousands of people year after year. All those people going through the turnstiles enabled fat purses to be offered, attracting cars and drivers from all over the United States. Those who towed from the West also had the advantage of the fall schedule to run at Reading and Williams Grove while they were in the area.

Hinnershitz finished fifth in the 30-lap feature on September 21, 1935, quite a respectable finish for his first outing at the fair oval. Allentown ran very few "still" dates—that term applies to non-fair races. This resulted in Hinnershitz receiving the chance to race and win there only once a year. He did finally win his first feature, a 20-lap event, on September 20, 1947. Hinnershitz went on to win eight times, and when he didn't win, he almost always ended the race among the top finishers. His phenomenal record at Allentown for 19 total appearances is 8 wins, two 2nd-place finishes, one 3rd-place, and three 5th-place finishes. The joy realized from all the success at the track was lessened considerably by the tragic death there of his good friend Johnny Thomson in 1960.

Joie Chitwood notched is only Allentown win on September 23, 1939, in the famed Chicago-based Hank O'Day Offenhauser. O'Day put Tony Willman in the car and returned to Allentown's victory circle on the still date July 6, 1940. Ted Horn won the fair race on September 21. Chitwood, back in the O'Day car now owned by machine shop owner Fred Peters, set fast time of 26.40 seconds when Horn won again in 1941 while many drivers were leaving AAA in favor of CSRA.

Jimmy Wilburn won the first race run after the end of World War

II, and AAA came back as the sanctioning organization at Allentown for the September 23, 1946, Bill Holland win.

The following fall after his first feature win, Hinnershitz began a successful run that lasted until his last race ever in 1960.

On September 20, 1952, Hinnershitz won his third Allentown feature in his own blue #1 Offenhauser. However, the day is best remembered for the grisly crash that took the life of Bill Schindler. An axle assembly came loose from a slower car and was struck by Schindler, who was in Earl Beal's Offy, causing the car to catapult through the backstretch fence and into a tree outside the track. A track worker outside the speedway was injured. Schindler was decapitated and killed instantly.

George "Dutch" Culp and Harry "Hack" Brown promoted races at Allentown beginning with a race on July 7, 1956. Hinnershitz won the 30-lap feature and set a new track record for 30 laps and for his 10-lap heat win. He came back on September 22 and won the 20-lap Allentown Fair Sweepstakes, and the next day, he did it one more time at the Reading Fair, winning the 20-lap main event beating back a terrific threat from Midwestern newcomer Jud Larson. Johnny Thomson and Los Angeles driver Van Johnson followed Larson. Larson set a new one-lap track record of 23.95 seconds, breaking the late Wally Campbell's three-year-old mark of 24.12 seconds. In his heat race, Hinnershitz went on to set a new eight-lap record of 3:23.52 minutes, breaking Danny Kladis' 1955 record of 3:25.48 minutes.

Chapter 9

The Big Time

A baseball player knows he's reached the big time when he gets to play in the World Series. A football quarterback knows he's reached the big time when he gets to play in the Super Bowl. And let's not forget the athletes who fulfill their dreams by competing in the Olympic Games. Race drivers know they've reached the big time when they race in the Indianapolis 500. Those who have started the Indianapolis 500 are members of a group recognized as very special.

During the time Hinnershitz raced at Indianapolis, it took an awesome amount of physical and mental endurance. Man-handling the racecars of those days at such high speeds required substantial muscular strength. In the *early years*, it took much longer to race 500 miles. Exhaustion and dehydration were common occurrences, and relief drivers were frequently used when the starting driver needed a break or couldn't continue.

Hinnershitz was a spectator at Indianapolis seven times beginning in 1924. He was destined to race there, and in 1939, he passed his rookie test. His first year there had mixed results. He easily passed his rookie test, but he couldn't get the Offenhauser-powered Kimmel Special up to qualifying speed. Qualifying trials back then were 10 laps. According to Hinnershitz, warming up at 80 or 90 miles per hour on the tires used in those days was so bumpy it actually blurred a driver's vision. The turns were paved, but the straight-aways were brick. When drivers got their speed up to 130 or 135 miles per hour, things got a little better.

He returned in 1940, this time in the Offenhauser-powered Marks Special and qualified it in the ninth starting spot. On lap 32 of the race, he hit the front stretch concrete, bouncing off the wall several times and spinning wildly. He ended up in the infield at the first turn. He fractured his right wrist as a result of the crash, caused by the rear wheels locking up. Wilbur Shaw went on to win the 1940 race.

In 1941 he qualified the Marks car in the 20th starting position. In spite of the car vibrating during most of the race, he finished 10th, running the entire 500 miles. He was relieved by George Robson. Mauri Rose won the race that year, driving relief for starter Floyd Davis.

Hinnershitz's return in 1946 was disappointing. Because of a broken driveshaft, he failed to qualify a Maserati-powered car owned by Milt Marion. Hinnershitz skipped Indianapolis in 1947. A deal to drive a car owned by Ted Horn never materialized.

Edward J. Walsh, Jr. would have indirect influence on Hinnershitz's driving at Indianapolis. Walsh was a millionaire investor who started driving racecars in 1927. He developed into a competent driver and became especially successful driving Midgets. Of course, like so many men, his dream was to race in the Indianapolis 500. He might have very well attained that dream had it not been for becoming an owner of the car Johnnie Parsons drove to victory in the 1950 Indianapolis 500, the same car Hinnershitz drove in the 1948 race. Walsh's money became more useful and fruitful to his career in auto-racing than his driving talent.

Walsh not only had money; he was of "blue blood." Born in St. Louis in 1909, he was a descendent of Rene Chouteau, one of the founders of that city in 1764. He took his first trip to Indianapolis in 1927 when he was 18 years old. When he returned home, he began racing Model Ts but gave up driving in 1937 when he got married.

Walsh went to Indianapolis in 1938 to be a car owner and leased an Offenhauser powered Stevens chassis that Bill Cummings drove in the 1932 race. Car builder Myron Stevens, a master sheet metal man who had worked for Harry Miller, built the car. Practically all Millers carried Myron Stevens's bodywork—he was head of the Miller body shop all through the 1920s.

With Billy DeVore behind the wheel, the car qualified a dismal 30th. Surprisingly, when the race was over, DeVore drove the car to an eighth-place finish. Walsh considered this first venture very successful. In 1939 he returned with a Stevens-built Miller-powered car. This car was famous, although Walsh didn't know it or care. It had been stored at Harry Miller's Los Angeles garage since 1933 while Miller fought off bankruptcy. When Miller's business finally failed brothers Frank and Al Scully bought the car. The Scullys gave the ride to Peter DePaolo and took it to Europe to run in several races.

When the Scullys brought the car back to Los Angeles, they tore it apart. The chassis was sold to Lou Moore who put Fred Frame in the car. Frame finished 32nd in the 1936 Indianapolis 500 when the Miller engine failed. Jack Holly bought the car to run in the 1938 race, installed an Offenhauser engine in it, and gave the ride to Al Miller. Miller finished 18th.

In 1939 Walsh bought the car and gave Floyd Davis the driving job. Davis qualified in the 29th position and finished 27th after a shock absorber failed. Davis would win the race two years later, but not in an Ed Walsh owned car.

Just before the 1939 race, Walsh met a young Frank Kurtis. Kurtis was working on repairing a wrecked car driven by DeVore. Walsh was so impressed with Kurtis, he asked him to go to St. Louis with him to work on and improve his car. Kurtis wound up rebuilding the Miller car and working for Walsh's crew during the 1940 Indianapolis 500.

Kurtis was born in 1908. His trademark was "race car designer." He designed the car and then built it. He didn't build copies. He created sports cars, Midgets, Sprint cars, and Championship and Formula I cars. His career began when he was hired to fabricate Midget car bodies, and then in the late 1930s, he started building his own Midget cars after settling in California. In addition to building over 500 race-ready Midgets, he created the Kurtis-Kraft Kit. Racers could buy a Kurtis Midget in pieces and put it together in their own shop.

His Midgets were equipped with a smaller version of the Offenhauser motor and were practically unbeatable for over two decades. He created about 120 Championship cars, including five Indianapolis 500 winners.

Kurtis built Walsh a new car in 1941, using many parts from the old car. In the 1941 race, Sam Hanks qualified the car in the 32nd spot and then crashed it during practice when the crankshaft broke. Kurtis took the wrecked car back to Los Angeles, where it sat in his garage until the war was over. Walsh sold the car after the 1947 race.

In the 1946 race, with George Connor in the cockpit, the car ran 38 laps before a piston broke. In the 1947 race the car ran 32 laps before the fuel tank began to leak. Walsh's money wasn't buying too much success at the time. Soon after, Walsh and Kurtis decided to enter a partnership. Walsh was to provide the money and Kurtis the expertise. Kurtis got a paycheck, and the two men split the profits evenly.

The Indianapolis car Kurtis envisioned finally arrived at the Indianapolis Motor Speedway in May of 1948. He named it the Kurtis-Kraft Special. It featured four-wheel independent suspension and other innovations, including a rubberized fuel tank to prevent the tank from splitting during a crash. Kurtis hired Walt Brown to drive it. Brown had finished seventh in the 1947 point standings.

During practice at the Arlington Downs, Texas 100-miler, a component of the rear suspension broke, necessitating Kurtis to hurry the car back to California for repairs. He replaced the casting with a fabricated steel part. At Indianapolis, Brown couldn't get the car up to qualifying speed. He couldn't seem to get comfortable with the new suspension system on the car and probably expressed concern about a repeat of the problem at Arlington.

Kurtis turned to Hinnershitz, whom he knew was primarily a dirt track driver with little experience on pavement. But he also realized Hinnershitz was a driver who used his head and had substantial natural talent. Hinnershitz possessed a reputation for being able to quickly adapt to mechanical or track conditions. That was important. He would have to adapt to the Kurtis-Kraft independent suspension system Brown wasn't able to do.

Hinnershitz qualified the car in the 23rd starting spot and was amazingly running fourth when the car developed magneto problems. More amazing is the fact that Hinnershitz spent many precious minutes in the pits while Kurtis and his crew tried to fix the magneto, and after re-entering the race, he still went on to finish ninth, only two laps down. Hinnershitz was able to make the Kurtis car go fast on the bricks, and as a result he brought home the bacon. The ninth-place finish paid $4,270. Hinnershitz's share was $1,700, quite a bit of money at that time. It was his best chance to win the Indianapolis 500. Without the contrary magneto, there was an excellent chance he would have ended the afternoon in victory circle.

Given Hinnershitz's rare and natural talent recognized by car owners like Kurtis, his future at Indianapolis and in the Championship car division looked bright. Many experts agree that if it had not been for the mechanical problems Hinnershitz experienced, he would have joined that exclusive club of winners of the Indianapolis 500.

Despite a job offer by Kurtis, Hinnershitz elected to run a full Sprint car schedule. He felt much safer and more comfortable driving a Sprint car, and he really never liked running on the bricks. The primary reason Hinnershitz didn't like racing at Indianapolis was something going wrong and the banging starting before he had time to recover. He felt that on dirt he usually could figure out a way to get back in shape. Another factor that influenced his decision— Betty had always supported him in his driving career, but she didn't like Indianapolis and was happy when he decided not to run there anymore.

Consequently, Kurtis put Brown, who had new-found confidence running the car, back in it, and a week after Hinnershitz finished at Indianapolis with it, Brown qualified the car 10th on the dirt at Milwaukee on June 6. He finished in 13th spot. On June 20, he won with the car at Langhorne.

Kurtis put his mechanic Harry Stephens in charge of the car, and he made plans to head back to California. Later in the season, Stephens gave West Coast-charger Johnnie Parsons the ride. Parsons won the race in the car at DuQuoin the day Ted Horn was killed. Stephens, happy with Parson's performance, kept him in the car for the 1949 season. Parsons had a very good year, including a second-place finish behind winner Bill Holland in the Indianapolis 500. The following year, Parsons did what fate denied Hinnershitz the opportunity to do. He put the car in victory circle, winning the rain-shortened 1950 Indianapolis 500.

The night before the race, Stephens discovered the car had a cracked engine block. Experiencing the intense disappointment and frustration that only the Indianapolis Motor Speedway can bestow to a racing team, Stephens told Parsons to get out front and lead the race for as many laps as he can before the engine gives. The lap money, earned by the leader of each lap, would be their only chance to make any money. Parsons did what he was told to do. While all the faster cars held back, pacing themselves for a long 500-mile race, Parsons moved far out front and was leading the pack when it started to rain. The race was red-flagged on the 138th lap, and Parsons was proclaimed the winner.

Chapter 10

A New Champion

In 1949 Tommy Hinnershitz was crowned the AAA Eastern Sprint car champion. He had driven primarily Ted Horn's rail-frame car, which had been built for high-banked speedways, successfully enough to earn the crown. He drove the car with the shorter wheelbase Bob Blake had built him on the regular half-mile tracks. Rail-frame Sprint cars were built on production frames, the same type of frame used by Detroit for conventional automobiles.

In 1949 he turned to master car builder Hiram Hillegass and ordered a new car. Hillegass would build a car of revolutionary design that would enable Hinnershitz to compete using his unique driving style. Using aircraft building methods, Hillegass built a car with a tubular chassis and a spring front and rear. It became Hinnershitz's all-time favorite. By this time, he had developed a driving style of artistic finess, driving smoothly, fast, and high in the turns, and he needed a car built with ground-breaking engineering that would be able to support his revolutionary driving style. Hinnershitz was convinced Hillegass could do the job. He won the 1950, 1951, and 1952 Eastern AAA Sprint car title in that car and drove it to a second place finish in the 1953 standings behind Joe Sostilio.

During the winter of 1953 Hinnershitz ordered another Hillegass car, this time with a torsion bar rear and a spring front. His confidence in Hillegass was solid. Hinnershitz realized that success in auto-racing, including dirt track racing, was depending more and more on building a race car that could be set up; adjusting weight distribution to be competitive at each individual racetrack under differing and constantly changing circumstances. The tube-framed Hillegass cars with torsion bars were being built with this flexible set-up in mind. Of course, gearing was also an important factor, along with experimenting with tire stagger.

These were the times when a driver was much more of a factor in how a racecar handled. Hinnershitz's driving style was different from Ted Horn's, or Mike Nazurak's, or Rex May's. A racecar could be set up to be driven for a particular driver, but the set-up might need to be changed considerably when another driver got into the car.

In the era of dirt tracks and day racing, as opposed to clay ovals under track lights, weather was an even more important factor. Most chassis men kept a book for each track the car competed at. The next year when they returned, they could look back and see how they set up the car the previous year. It saved a lot of time.

Hillegass began building racecars in 1919 while working for Mack Trucks in Allentown. By the time his career ended, he was recognized as one of the most talented and successful builders of racecars. He primarily built Midgets during their high popularity in the 1930s. Hillegass had been living in Syracuse working a research and development job until after the war. He returned to Allentown and set up shop at 2435 South Fourth Street.

He developed a strong, lightweight tube frame and the sheet metal to go over it. He built three Sprint cars in 1949 and three more in 1950. One of them was built for Hinnershitz. The price tag for a Hillegass car was $925. Before long the car owners who had successfully campaigned Hillegass Midgets on one-third and one-quarter-mile tracks were demanding the bigger Sprint cars to run on half-mile tracks.

Hillegass made car building a viable business. He, like many of his contemporaries, was looking for alternatives to the old production car rail-frames that had been used to build the pre-war racecars. With knowledge acquired from the aircraft defense industry, car builders began to use high strength steel tubing as frame rails. The tube frame caught on quickly. With so many adopting steel tubing, Hillegass needed to develop his own unique style, and it turned out to be very compatible with the Hinnershitz style.

Hinnershitz's AAA Eastern Sprint championships in 1949 and 1950 were won in the old Horn production rail-frame car. In 1951, his first season with the new Hillegass car, Hinnershitz captured the title once again. However, he experienced many problems with the car. Getting off to a slow start for the new season, he asked for advice from some of the Midget drivers who were running Kurtis tube cars, comparable to Hinnershitz's Hillegass Sprint car. Their input didn't help. He even considered going back to the old Horn car. The sixth race on the schedule was at Williams Grove, and he finally won a feature. Whether it was just finding the right set-up, or Hinnershitz feeling more comfortable with the car, one supposes success came from an unknown messenger. Now that he had the car dialed in, he came back in 1952 to win his fourth championship.

After Hinnershitz bought the second Hillegass car during the winter of 1953 Miracle Power Products signed on as a national sponsor.

Hinnershitz made some major changes to the car, once again practicing that amazing ability to think things out in his mind differently from everyone else. In this particular case, he utilized the Hillegass shop and then personally did the mechanical work necessary to implement his changes. Hinnershitz moved the engine further back in the car and made some improvements on the suspension. He has not received wide recognition for mechanical innovation because of his hesitancy to claim credit for most of his contributions to racecar engineering. He became proficient working on Offenhauser engines—tearing down, rebuilding, and otherwise maintaining the power source used in his racecar and most other Championship, Sprint, and Midget cars racing with AAA.

Fred Offenhauser (1888-1973) was an automotive engineer and mechanic who designed the Offenhauser racing engine, nicknamed the "Offy." Offenhauser began working for Harry Miller in 1913 when he was 25 years old. A little while later Miller put him in charge of the engine department. That year was a very good year at

Indianapolis for Frenchmen. Jules Goux won the 1913 Indianapolis 500 in a French made Peugot Grand Prix car powered by a state of the art double overhead cam four valve per cylinder engine. Because of World War I, car owner Bob Burma found it impossible to get parts, so Burma brought the car to Miller's shop to be maintained. Offenhauser was assigned the job.

Learning all about the Peugeot engine while working on it enabled Offenhauser to design, develop, and build the Miller racing engine, which led to the Offenhauser racing engine. Later on, in 1917, Offenhauser proved he could be innovative and willing and able to work on experimental projects when he designed and built Barney Oldfield's famous "Golden Submarine" in the Miller shop.

In 1919 designer Leo Goossen (1895-1974) was hired by Miller, and Offenhauser became plant manager. Goossen's job was to put Miller and Offenhauser's ideas on to paper, figure out the technical requirements, and prepare drawings required for construction. It was an ideal environment for the young draftsman to work in. Offenhauser's talent running the factory and Miller's dreams, imagination, and his confidence in Goossen to create drawings that could be translated into perfect racing machinery, made for a formidable operation.

Around 1930 a racecar owner put one of Miller's four-cylinder, 151-cubic-inch displacement marine engines in one of his racecars. This prototype surpassed all expectations when it powered the racecar to set a new international speed record of 144.895 miles per hour. The marine engine was then developed into a twin-cam, four-valve, 220 cubic inch displacement, four-cylinder auto-racing engine. In spite of its potential, Miller wasn't interested in developing it, but Offenhauser was.

When Miller went bankrupt in 1933, Offenhauser bought the patterns and equipment and began refining the engine with Goossen. It was the beginning of the "Offy" dynasty. The Offenhauser four-cylinder engines attained overwhelming success, dominating Sprint car and Championship car racing from 1934 to 1960, including 24 Indianapolis wins in 27 years. The success of Offenhauser's engines lay in the fact that they produced staggering outputs of up to three horsepower per cubic inch. During all those years, Offenhauser seldom showed up at speedways.

Offenhauser sold the business in 1946 to Louis Meyer and Dale Drake. Meyer and Drake continued producing the motor using the Offenhauser name. Goossen stayed on with the new owners.

Chapter 11

Building a Legacy

The 1950s were fruitful years for Hinnershitz. He won championships, defended the crowns more than once, and extended what became a long tenure as a successful car owner. During the week, he farmed. He was, like his ancestors, a farmer all his life. He grew corn, wheat, oats, and hay. He had a cow or two, some beef cattle, and at various times raised sheep and chickens. The family garden was nearly one acre, the source of the string beans Betty jarred each year. He worked on the race car just a few feet from the house in the "garage," which was actually the upper level of the bank barn renovated to accommodate a full-fledged racecar operation—Hinnershitz racing headquarters.

He had a loyal crew. Hinnershitz called them his helpers; Charles Nuss, Ken (Red) Schaeffer, John Spayd, and Cliff Nein stuck with Hinnershitz through the years. They were like uncles to the Hinnershitz daughters, Jeanne, born in 1939, and Carol, born in 1943. Whenever possible, there was a picnic at the farm for the family and crewmembers after the races. It was an idyllic lifestyle, a peaceful family-oriented existence during the week without fame or glamour that Hinnershitz never really took seriously. The end of each day always included the family eating the evening meal together.

Hinnershitz and his family weren't Amish or Mennonite; they

were mainstream Pennsylvania Dutch of German ancestry who could easily blend in with people walking down 42nd Street in New York City. However, before the advent of television in the early 1950s, which introduced all Americans to a broader view of the world, many Pennsylvania Dutch chose to live within an environment of rich ethnic culture that featured foods, language, and other customs that could be difficult for outsiders to penetrate.

During the winters, it was calm and quiet at the farm for Hinnershitz and the family. In the garage, he worked on his racecar while the girls went to school and Betty kept house and held a job outside the home. The crewmembers were there to help.

When spring and then summer and fall weekends arrived the sedate lifestyle on the farm was replaced by travel and the excitement of racing. Racing not only thrilled the lives of thousands of race fans, it electrified the family, friends, and crewmembers. At the end of each week during racing season, Hinnershitz and a crewmember would tow the racecar up to the end of the dirt lane, push it off, and fire it up. After working on the engine during the week, he would have to fine-tune it for the upcoming weekend of racing. At one time, he had given some serious thought to building a test track on the farm but never followed through on that idea.

He wasn't superstitious, but he did fear being burned to death while racing. When Betty decided to wear a green dress to the races, he insisted she change, possibly reasoning it would appear she was making fun of those who believed the color green was bad luck. He discouraged his superstitious competitors from borrowing his tools—he painted them green.

To make himself and a crewmember or two more comfortable while keeping travel expenses low, he built an attractive sheet metal cap over the back of the pick-up truck. Inside he built two levels. On the top level was placed a wide mattress; the tools were kept on the lower level. Sandwiches were packed, skipping restaurants to save money. Hammering together accommodations and packing provisions showcased Hinnershitz's ability to innovate and travel lean. Another example was the full-face shield he developed, an item he probably could have patented. He crafted prototypes and loaned them to other drivers.

Hinnershitz and his crewmembers made grueling trips, especially when they raced out west. Those were the days before interstate highways; in most areas there were no highways at all, just mile after mile of two-lane blacktop roads passing through large cities, small villages, up hills, down hills, and over narrow and dilapidated bridges. On the trailer being pulled by the Dodge pick-up was that gleaming, brightly painted and chromed Sprint car.

When racing was not far from home, Betty and the girls followed in the car. When they were at Williams Grove, the girls spent the day at the amusement park while their father did his job next door on the half-mile speedway. On one occasion while traveling through Laureldale on the way to Williams Grove, for some reason the race car bounced off the trailer into a couple of parked cars. There was no time for long conferences. After a brief exchange of information with the owners of the damaged cars, the Hinnershitz family and crew were off to the races.

Serving as a preamble to the 1950s, the 1949 season was good to Hinnershitz overall, but he did get knocked around a bit. He started off by winning the inaugural 25-lap event in April at Reading, but later in the month, he hit the wall at Indianapolis during practice and suffered head injuries.

Three days later, on April 24, he won the 30-lap feature at Williams Grove and went on to win features at Heidelberg and Bedford, Pennsylvania; Middletown, New York; St. Paul, Minnesota; Richmond, Virginia; and Owego, New York, and another win each at Williams Grove and at Reading, Hinnershitz won the title in 1950 in fine style, running up front and winning features while racing a busy, full schedule. However, on July 4th is when he flipped at Lakewood Park in Atlanta. He was admitted to the hospital where it was discovered he suffered a fractured pelvis. He was back in the cockpit though on the July 29, when he finished second in the feature at Harrington, Delaware.

Chapter 12

Dog Day at the Races

The "Dog Day at the Races" occurred on May 9, 1955, at Williams Grove. To many people, it sounds comical, and in a way it was. An incident during the afternoon program consisted of racecar drivers skillfully avoiding what could have been a tragedy.

Everything seemed normal as the field for the feature race was coming out of the fourth turn ready to take the start. The green flag was waved, and as expected, everyone tried to get into the first turn before everybody else. All of a sudden, a dog came out of nowhere and started running across the track in the second turn.

Six of the 12 drivers to start the 30-lap feature got tangled up coming out of the second turn. Al Herman, who was on the pole, moved to avoid hitting the dog. Hinnershitz also moved out of the way but rode up over Herman's wheel. Both of them spun as the field came roaring out of the turn and on to the backstretch. They were like sitting ducks. Eddie Johnson of Akron, Ohio, in the Leitenberger Offy rode up over the tail of Al Keller. Just three weeks later Keller would be involved in the crash during the 1955 Indianapolis 500 that killed Billy Vukovich.

The melee was far from over. Allentown's Buster Warke, in Dutch Culp's car that day, destroyed a portion of the Grove's fence. The car didn't fare too well; it suffered a bent axle.

With Hinnershitz still sitting there helpless alongside Herman, Johnny Thomson crashed into the growing pile of Sprint cars. Thomson and Herman's cars wound up with bent radius rods. Keller's car escaped with a bent tail while Hinnershitz and Johnson's cars didn't receive any damage.

The red flag was thrown, halting the race. While a variety of track workers repaired the fence, removed racecars and cleaned up the mess, AAA officials ruled that Thomson, Herman, and Warke couldn't restart because their cars needed to be magna-fluxed. AAA rules stated that any car damaged in an accident must be magna-fluxed before it can be competed again. Magna-fluxing is a system whose functions and purposes can be compared somewhat to an X-ray. It detects any cracks in a racecar's frame and the parts that are bolted to the frame and become part of the racecar.

As expected, the fans roared in protest, and after the officials conferred, they reversed their original ruling and allowed the three to restart the race.

It turned out to be another Hinnershitz victory, followed by Thomson in another Sam Traylor owned car; then came Herman, Keller, Hank Rogers, Ernie McCoy, and Charlie Musselman. By the 18th lap of the 30-lap feature, Hinnershitz started to lap the rear of the field just as Johnson spun out in the second turn, losing his chance to finish the feature. He didn't hit anyone or anything, sparing his car any damage. Because of his bent radius rod, Herman experienced major handling problems throughout the race. Thomson finally took second spot away from him on lap 13. Warke never did finish the race. He was forced to drop out on the 24th lap when his brakes caught fire.

Who the dog's owner was, where the dog came from, and what were the circumstances surrounding the animal running loose at a sporting event with speeding racecars being attended by thousands of people remained a mystery.

The 35-year-old Keller from upstate New York started racing in modified stock cars. A year before the dog incident, competing in NASCAR, he won driving a Hudson at Savannah, Georgia. He switched to Sprint cars, driving for Sam Traylor. That's the ride that brought him to Williams Grove that day in May 1955.

Meanwhile, Traylor acquired an ex-Rex Mays Championship car, and Keller was given the ride for the 1955 Indianapolis 500. It was during that race Keller was involved in the crash that claimed the life of Bill Vukovich. Vukovich was exiting the second turn, trailing three slower cars being driven by Rodger Ward, Johnny Boyd, and Keller. When Ward's car swerved as the result of a wind gust, Keller swerved into the infield to avoid Ward, then lost control of the car and slid back on to the track, striking Boyd's car and pushing it into Vukovich's path. Years later, in 1961, Keller was killed in a Championship car at Phoenix.

Chapter 13

Tommy Hinnershitz Day

October 9, 1955 was Tommy Hinnershitz Day at the Reading Fairgrounds. Race Director Russ Moyer decided devoting an entire race day to honor the local racing hero was in order. A large crowd turned out to see Hinnershitz honored by city, county, and Reading Fair officials, including Fair President John S. Giles. Hinnershitz was showered with gifts, including a brand new blue 1956 Dodge, a shotgun, shirts, trophies, $250 from the Reading Fair, and a beautiful scroll from the Reading-Berks Chamber of Commerce. Mildred Kerns, a trustee of the Checkered Flag Fan Club, presented the keys to the car to Hinnershitz, who then took his family for a lap around the track while the crowd cheered.

Eddie Sachs won the 50-lap feature. Hinnershitz, finishing second, got a little carried away, almost flipping a few times. The unusually rough fall weather created rough track conditions, rare for Reading, causing the car's shock absorbers to fail around lap 24, resulting in Hinnershitz's physical beating for the rest of the race. Both Hinnershitz and Sachs lapped the entire remaining 14-car field. Hinnershitz raced especially hard to show his appreciation to the fans for honoring him. He retained the point lead over Charlie Mussleman, who finished eighth.

Finishing behind Hinnershitz were Mike Magill of Haddonfield,

New Jersey; Danny Kladis in the Pfrommer Offy; Joe Barzda in the Culp Offy; Jiggs Peters, Plainfield, New Jersey; Lucky Loux of Quakertown, Pennsylvania; and Mussleman. Loux and Mussleman were driving Sam Traylor owned Offys. Hinnershitz started on the pole and bolted to the lead, but the track conditions forced him to let up. Sachs took the lead from him on lap 31 and went on to widen his lead in the final 19 laps.

It was a special day honoring the great dirt tracker. Now his home track, the famed Reading Fairgrounds half-mile oval would be put to sleep for the winter. The bleachers were disassembled and put away. As late as 1957, the uncovered seats were stored away to protect them from the harsh winter weather.

Chapter 14

The Nyquist Offy

In the *early years*, racecars had histories and their own distinct identities. They weren't bolted together from parts here and there to race at a different track on a different day. Racecars seemed to have a personality of their own. Just as a jockey needs to know the horse he's riding in a particular race, the smart racecar driver wants to know a racecar's peculiarities, what he can and can't do with it.

The Nyquist Offy, owned by former driver Ted Nyquist of Reading, had become a catastrophe by the time Hinnershitz later climbed into it. Despite the fact the car was built by the brilliant Hiram Hillegass and well maintained by Nyquist, it had a rough going. Probably the biggest reason the Nyquist Offy was entangled in so much misfortune was because it was too good of a racecar. Nyquist and his crew did a superb job of maintaining the chassis set-up and the Offenhauser engine. It was fast and willing to go exactly where the driver decided to plant it. It gave the driver sitting in it a huge feeling of self-confidence.

In 1954, when the car was two years old, the young and reckless Wally Campbell died in it at Salem, Indiana. Campbell, born in 1926, began racing midgets in 1947 with ARDC and then switched to stockcars. He was the 1951 NASCAR national modified stock car champion. In 1952 he tried out the grand-national division, winning the pole for the Darlington 500 while also racing his own Sprint car with URC.

Success was coming to Campbell fast. After campaigning with URC in 1953, he moved to AAA for the 1954 season. While driving a Frank Kurtis Sprint car, Sam Traylor offered Campbell a Sprint car ride and the opportunity to drive one of the Traylor Championship cars. Traylor knew Campbell had fast reflexes and was fearless, but he also knew he could be wild. At Indianapolis, AAA officials told Campbell he needed more experience and sent him home after he drove erratically during his rookie test.

Campbell wanted to learn how to win on the high banks in the Midwest, but Traylor didn't want to send a Sprint car out there, so Campbell somehow got Nyquist to give him a ride. A special practice session was arranged for Saturday, July 18, 1954, at Salem Speedway with 1952 Indianapolis winner Troy Ruttman and Jiggs Peters standing by as members of a small group of advisors. Peters was a thinker when it came to setting up a racecar. When Jiggs drove racecars, he brought along a mounted white-wall passenger car tire that he insisted be put on the car's right front corner. For some reason, that set-up worked for him, and nobody asked any questions.

After Campbell completed about 40 hot laps, he took the car out over Salem's second turn, flying like an airplane and then falling down into the cornfield and setting it afire. The 28-year-old daredevil died in the fiery crash from multiple injuries.

Nyquist took the badly bent-up car home, pulled the engine and rear end, salvaged what he could, and then hired Hillegass to put together a new Nyquist Offy with a tube frame, four-wheel disk brakes, and a spring front and rear end. By this time, Hillegass's tube frames had gained a good reputation, the first one had been built in 1949 for Joe Mattera from Deer Lake, Pennsylvania. Joe and his wife Fran's Deer Lake Inn Restaurant was located just a mile or two from the camp where Mohammed Ali trained during his reign as world heavyweight boxing champion. The champ and his entourage stopped by. The Mercury engine-powered Sprint car christened the Deer Lake Inn Special was driven by Joe Mattera throughout the 1950s.

Just two months after Campbell's death on September 24, 1954,

Chicago driver Danny Kladis conquered the Allentown Fair half-mile in the new Nyquist car. Nyquist and his crew's outstanding work carried over to the new car. From the very beginning, the car handled exceptionally well, although unpredictable at times, and it was fast—awfully fast. Those characteristics would prove to be a lethal combination. Winter set in, with the Nyquist car only needing a little freshening up to be ready for spring 1955. The car's 1955 sponsor was the Pfrommer Trucking Company. Company owner John Pfrommer would eventually buy the car.

Mike Nazaruk, born in 1921 in Newark, New Jersey, was killed at Langhorne Speedway in the newly rebuilt Nyquist Offy on May 1, 1955. He raced Midgets, Sprint cars, and Championship cars, including three starts in the Indianapolis 500. While serving as a Marine in World War II, Nazaruk promised himself that he would become a racecar driver. When he was discharged, he began racing Midgets. In 1947 he won the track championships at Staten Island and Rhinebeck, New York. In 1948 he scored over 20 feature wins at Middletown, New York, winning the 1948 track championship. It seemed his career was successfully moving along. In 1949 he was ARDC Midget champion.

Nazaruk joined AAA in 1950, and he won 14 national Midget events, including the 1950 "Night Before the 500" at Raceway Park in Indianapolis and the first Midget car race ever run at Terre Haute, Indiana, in 1953. He finished fifth in the 1954 AAA national Midget car points. He finished second in his rookie year in the 1951 Indianapolis 500. He competed two more times at Indianapolis, finishing 21st in 1953, forced out with mechanical problems, and 5th in 1954.

On that tragic day in May, 1955, Nazaruk became yet another victim of the treacherous Langhorne big circle. The race day program consisted of twin features. Fans were anxious to see "Iron Mike" master the dirt and oil surface. He was in the hottest car, and almost everyone knew it. While in the process of winning the first feature, he set a new track record. During the second feature, things went wrong, very wrong. Nazaruk flipped the Nyquist Offy violently numerous times and lost his life.

In July, the management of the Reading Fairgrounds decided to promote a Mike Nazaruk Memorial race, intended to be an annual 100-lap Sprint car event. On July 17, Al Herman was the first feature winner. Hinnershitz finished second in the race in his own Miracle Power Special. The following year, he won the 100-lap grind on June 10, 1956, and came back to finish third in the third annual race on June 16, 1957, won by Johnny Thomson.

On September 23, 1956, during the annual Reading Fair, Hinnershitz captured the 20-lap Fair Sweepstakes, fighting off a newcomer to the East making his Reading debut, Texas-born Jud Larson. The significance of Larson's second-place finish that fall day at Reading was the fact he did it in the unpredictable Nyquist Offy. Since Campbell and then Nazaruk were killed in it, numerous drivers had taken turns in the pilot's seat.

Larson, who during the 1950s raced wearing a T-shirt, had the raw talent needed to control the Nyquist car. He was just the man to force the Nyquist Offy to cooperate. He would manhandle a stubborn and reluctant racecar, running each lap differently and throwing it into the turns to put it exactly where he wanted to go.

On that September day in 1956, Larson drove the best he knew how just to keep up with the Miracle Power Special. Hinnershitz was in top form, having set a new eight-lap record while winning his heat. Larson set a new one-lap mark of 23.95 seconds, breaking Campbell's three-year-old record of 24.12 seconds.

Practically any car owner wanted Larson in their car despite his reputation for not showing up on race day. Driving racecars was as close to holding a job as he cared to be, and when he needed money, he was always fast. Thirty-three years old at the time, he spent the early years of his career racing all over the West and Midwest, competing at tracks in Texas, Oklahoma, Kansas and Iowa, racing often with IMCA. His record at Indianapolis was brief. He started 19th in 1958, finishing in 8th spot, and in 1959, he again started 19th but crashed in turn three on lap 45.

A fan favorite, Larson enjoyed signing autographs. He was one of racing's true gentlemen, a wonderful, happy-go-lucky man who loved life and people. One of his favorite stories he liked to tell was the time he was running up against the outside fence, assured that even a motorcycle didn't have enough room to get by him, when he looked over to his right and watched Hinnershitz drive by. Larson, like Hinnershitz, was a natural dirt track driver. Both of them had a distinctive style all their own. Larson tended to be more of a hard charger. He would set himself up to enter a turn by starting to get the racecar sideways as soon as he passed the starter's stand. Later, in the 1970s, Jan Opperman would mimic the Larson style.

The 50-Lap Mike Nazaruk Memorial Race

October 12, 1958, was one of the most amazing days ever at the Reading half-mile racetrack. The Nyquist Offy had been sold to trucking company owner John Pfrommer from Douglassville, Pennsylvania. Pfrommer recognized a golden opportunity when he saw it. After hearing the news that Hinnershitz sold the Miracle Power Special to racecar owner Herb Swan, Pfrommer signed Hinnershitz to drive the renamed Pfrommer Offy.

The 1958 version of the Mike Nazaruk Memorial Race was scaled back to a 50-lap feature event. A certain amount of uneasiness settled in throughout the packed, big steel and concrete grandstand that day. The legendary hometown boy was going to compete in the racecar that two race drivers died in, including the one that the race was named after. It was unavoidable that fans would be wary of another tragedy if the unpredictable car that Jud Larson controlled so well would decide to veto a driver's command.

The afternoon started off normal enough with Hinnershitz finishing third in his 10-lap heat. But that's when normal ended.

In the feature, he started going around everyone, got into the lead and started to pass lapped traffic. He passed Johnny Thomson, who was running in second spot, and in doing so lapped the entire field. Hinnershitz's run ended on the 40th lap when the racecar that some said had its own spirit decided to quit running.

Those who believe a racecar can have a spirit wondered if there was conflict between the Nyquist Offy and the drivers who died driving it. Did the car win the tragic battles that took the lives of Wally Campbell and Mike Nazaruk? Did Jud Larson show it once and for all that the driver rules? Many will say this is all nonsense, but the fact remains that on that October day in 1958, man won over machine. Hinnershitz raced it like it had never been raced before. Like a jockey who drops the reigns, he didn't hold back. He forced it to run as fast as it could. He raced it until it couldn't race anymore. Just like a horse that lays down exhausted and gasping for air after being forced to run until near death, the Pfrommer Offy sat still and alone on the backstretch under a settling blue haze of smoke.

Race victor Johnny Thomson said he was sure he was running second until he saw Hinnershitz drive by him. He assumed correctly; he was running second—he was running second twice.

Hinnershitz stayed on to drive and maintain the Pfrommer racecar, winning races and another Sprint car championship in 1959.

Chapter 15

High, Wide, and Handsome

When wanting to conjure up images of "life on the open range" and the free spirit of the brave and the daring men whom roamed there, American writers have often turned to "high, wide, and handsome." High and wide describes the freedom attained from unlimited space on the prairie, and handsome can mean "to act generously or graciously." In the 1800s, when they would take out a lively colt, the farmers and cowboys would say, "he feels his oats," and he comes down the road, "high, wide, and handsome." This is about as American as a phrase can be.

Tommy Hinnershitz had developed a unique driving style that for many years only he mastered. He roamed his range—up against the outside fence of the racetrack's turns where nobody else dared to go. He put the racecar into a broad-slide and with the steering wheel basically fixed, he feathered the throttle just enough to keep the car moving forward while sideways. That's how he did his roaming. Good track announcers, sportscasters and sportswriters would point out that his sliding and soaring was a "high, wide, and handsome" style he used to thrash his rivals. As the years went by, Hinnershitz became an ever more efficient racecar driver. It became more difficult to beat him as time went on.

All drivers become better after years of experience. Some never become good, but they are better than when they started. The ones that have natural talent usually put in the work necessary to let it develop. There are those that squander it. There are some that have the talent but don't have the desire. The adrenaline rush, some have more intense rushes than others, can become physically and mentally exhausting for many after years of campaigning. Then there are those that can't live without that rush. They can become victims, driving when they should be retired, taking chances that aren't within the realm of reasonable risk, or maybe trying to drink away the memories of past glory.

The showmanship displayed before and after the actual racing at the annual fair races was designed to entertain while stirring up the emotions of the paying public. Hinnershitz became an example of hero worship; he was a promoter's dream. Fans picked him as their favorite because he was the only driver to race up against the outside fence. For new fans, he became their favorite as soon as the green flag waved during warm-ups. Fans driven to their feet by the excitement of seeing a legend, a sports icon, perform wondrous athletic skill has been a phenomenon reserved for only a select few like Hinnershitz.

He stood out as someone special even before he climbed into the car. The more observant picked him as their favorite before any racecars were pushed off—the Miracle Power Special was the most beautiful racecar there; its shiny chrome, glowing bright yellow and blue colors, and sparkling red number and lettering surpassed the beauty of all the other machines.

People, who for various reasons were privileged to be in the staging area, reached out to shake his hand as he walked from the pits to the racecar sitting silently on the front stretch waiting to be put to work. He was a man people wanted to touch and wish good luck.

In the *early years*, most fans got to see him only once a year at the state or county fair. The rest of the year, they had to settle for newspaper accounts with their black and white photographs. Perhaps they were lucky enough to have an autograph.

Throughout his career, he out-drove his competitors and his racecars out-performed the others. He almost always finished up front with the faster cars, and he won a lot of races. But there were other factors stirred into the ingredients that made Hinnershitz a *champion*. His competitiveness entailed more than just the acts of speed and style on the track. His ability to out-think the competition in original and unique ways created what perhaps in retrospect could have been given the moniker "The Hinnershitz Factor." It consisted of using shrewd strategy to get the slight edge because in auto-racing, seconds ticking on the stopwatch can mean the difference between a first and last place finish.

The strategy was almost always covert. Sometimes, after Hinnershitz made his pre-race walk around the track, he would crawl under the racecar and take the plate off the quick-change rear. Then he'd call out to one of his helpers to hand him particular gears. Other pit crewmembers would overhear and hurry back to their cars and install the same gears. Of course, Hinnershitz never installed the gears he called for. As a result, when the green flag was dropped for the feature, his car was geared just right, and the gears he called out to his crewmembers for were the worst ones to be using that day.

He thought out a plan for every race he entered. Part of his strategy was to be one of the first to take time trials. The more cars that ran on the track, the more slick or rough it would get, depending on the track's surface and reaction to the weather. Did it rain the day before? Was it a hot day with bright sunshine? Was it cool and cloudy? These were some of the questions Hinnershitz tried to answer logically instead of guessing.

Most times the heats were run inverted, but in the feature, the starting line-up was according to qualifying times—the fastest car sat on the pole. Hinnershitz knew there was less wear and tear on the car if he could qualify to start up front.

One race day at the Reading Fairgrounds, fans, officials, and other crew members watched in amazement as Hinnershitz's crew rolled rear tires down through the pits to the top of the front stretch, even though he, along with the entire field of cars, were lined up and parading around the track, all set for the green flag. As the cars gained speed coming out of the fourth turn, contemplating a start for the feature, Hinnershitz swerved out of line and pulled over next to the fence. The starter, unable to give the green flag, watched with dropped jaw as two tires and a jack were thrown over the fence followed by two crewmembers. The starter had no choice but to keep the field under yellow while the officials held a conference.

The track announcer, not forgetting that the fans are the people who were making the entire day possible, asked them whether the officials should wait for Hinnershitz. Thousands shouted, "Yes!" Hearing the thunderous message prompted the officials to allow him to fall into the rear of the field. That didn't satisfy the fans; consequently loud boos and other shouts of protest drowned out the announcer's explanation on the public address system.

The officials, realizing that the fans' shouting and booing were getting louder and a full scale riot was a real possibility, finally ruled Hinnershitz could start in his original spot. Now everything seemed to be back to normal, and the starter prepared to wave the green flag. There was one big difference. Hinnershitz's car had the right tires on to match the track conditions and the other cars didn't. They didn't know any better. Most didn't put the work into race preparation that Hinnershitz did. That's why they found the going a lot more difficult. That's why Hinnershitz won more races than any of them. When he suspected officials might make rulings against him, an extra helper or two were planted in the stands. They were experienced at stirring up fan protests. One famous incident at Williams Grove had fans actually climbing up the starter's stand.

Passing always depended on the other drivers. Hinnershitz knew where the drivers would be running on a particular race day just by observing the track conditions. The veteran drivers were predictable; he just needed to overpower and out-drive them. However, some of the young new drivers needed to be watched with caution in case one of them got into trouble and wasn't able to recover. It would take Hinnershitz a few laps to set up a rival and then wait for just the right opportunity to pass him. Patience and skill are usually more effective in Sprint car racing than using just power.

The driving style Hinnershitz developed was never copied during his career. When entering a turn, getting the back end of the car to break loose at the right time was essential. Doing that and still coming off the turns with maximum speed was critical. The best way to maintain the necessary speed was to find the high groove and use it lap after lap. Many drivers were done in by not being able to find that groove. There was also an inside groove, especially on hard slick tracks. That's where most drivers ran.

Hinnershitz ran high, wide, and handsome because there was less traffic and dust up against the outside. Less traffic meant more room to go fast; less dust meant better visibility.

He always admitted he didn't have the patience to push a driver, wait for him to make a mistake, and then go under him. That wasn't his style. He chose to run where others didn't dare to go. Races were won. New track records were set. Hinnershitz raced all over the country, but his biggest victories were always back home, at the local Pennsylvania tracks—the Reading Fairgrounds and Williams Grove Speedway, and years earlier, at the Lebanon Fairgrounds.

Chapter 16

A New and Safer Era

At the end of the 1955 racing season, AAA abruptly ceased sanctioning auto-racing events. The organization was increasingly busy providing services to motorists and going into the travel agency business. But these projects weren't the ultimate reason for the departure.

AAA was being criticized for its involvement in an activity that was causing death and injury almost on a weekly basis during the racing season. People were even prodding politicians to pass laws banning auto-racing. Many didn't consider it a sport.

For AAA and the sport of auto-racing, 1955 was not a good year. It was a year full of tragedy. First, Larry "Crash" Crockett, the 1954 Indianapolis 500 "Rookie of the Year," was killed in a Sprint car at Langhorne on March 20. On May 1, Langhorne snatched veteran Mike Nazaruk's life from the Nyquist car. On May 16, Manual Ayulo died at Indianapolis in practice, and then two-time winner Bill Vukovich, en-route to his third-straight 500 win, was killed on the 57th lap while leading the Indianapolis 500. It wasn't over yet, because the week after Indianapolis, Pierre Levegh's Mercedes plunged into the stands at Le Mans. In July, Indianapolis pole sitter Jerry Hoyt was killed in a Sprint car at Oklahoma City, Oklahoma. Finally, on November 6, Indianapolis veteran Jack McGrath was killed on the 1-mile dirt track at Phoenix.

AAA had for years enforced their rules, many of them petty, with unrelenting efficiency. But it failed miserably when it came to safety. It buckled under pressure from owners, mechanics, and drivers, failing to take steps to make racing safer. AAA officials, many of them former competitors, cooperated and agreed with the belief that no amount of safety precautions would decrease the chances of injuries, and in some cases, death.

Joie Chitwood was the first driver to use a seat belt at Indianapolis. It caused quite a stir. Chitwood didn't use the seat belt to keep him in the racecar in the event he got upside down. Chitwood used the seat belt to prevent him from bouncing around in the car while he ran on the bricks on the straight-aways. He bounced so much he had a difficult time keeping his foot on the throttle.

In those days, it was believed a racecar driver had a better chance of survival if he was thrown from the car. Consequently, in order to get permission to use the seat belt, Chitwood had to promise the officials that as soon as he realized he was going to be involved in an accident, he would unbuckle the belt so he would be thrown clear. Resistance to the introduction of any safety equipment was firmly entrenched in the minds of everyone involved with auto-racing.

Tommy Hinnershitz always said his biggest fear was being burned in a crash. While fire was a serious threat, especially with the use of gasoline as fuel in fuel tanks that contained no bladder, the most likely way a driver would lose his life was receiving a fractured skull, broken neck, or even being decapitated when flipping the car, especially if it landed on top of him. Hinnershitz had his share of scrapes when he was beginning his career, but by the time the 1950s arrived, Sprint cars were going faster, and driver's serious injuries and fatalities were mounting as speeds and the amount of racing nationwide increased.

Starting in 1956, when USAC was founded, two inevitable and significant thresholds needed to be crossed in Sprint car racing. The first was the requirement that all Sprint cars have roll bars. Many people resisted, convinced roll bars took away from the aesthetics of the cars, the first step taken to destroy the unique appearance of a Sprint car.

Consequently, Hinnershitz only had the benefit of a roll bar the last three years he raced. Sprint car racing was becoming faster and more aggressive. The injuries and deaths that drove AAA out of racing were only going to get worse if some steps toward increased safety weren't taken.

Chevrolet-powered Sprint cars that were brought east by drivers including A.J. Foyt, Jim Hurtibuise, Parnelli Jones, Johnny White, and others, allowed a more aggressive style of racing. More powerful cars were indications of a new era in dirt track racing, especially on the half-mile tracks. The death of Johnny Thomson was perhaps precipitated by seeking to be competitive driving an Offenhauser powered machine that was incapable of matching the power of the Chevrolets, especially coming off the turns.

Hinnershitz's decision to announce his retirement that fall day in 1960 at Allentown was made for a number or reasons. First, the death of his friend Thomson certainly had an affect on him. Also, his hands, with a touch of arthritis, were bothering him. Some could say Hinnershitz became obsolete that day or that he "saw the handwriting on the wall." But he had not yet become the old man who couldn't keep up with the young boys. He had met up with Foyt and some of those other new guys out in the Midwest before that day; he could run quite well with them and could be just as aggressive. He did his share of beating them.

What really transpired for Hinnershitz was he realized he had more success than any athlete could ever wish for; he had his reputation and dignity intact, and he had accomplished over the years what he had set out to accomplish. His official record spoke for itself. It was time for him to pass the torch to the next generation, just like the torch was passed to him by Ted Horn, John Gerber, Dutch and Parke Culp, Johnny Hannon, and others. He had the respect of the new upcoming drivers, so he quit. He had always made good decisions; making the decision to quit was a good and wise choice.

The second Sprint car threshold that needed to be crossed was, by the late 1960s, the need to put cages on Sprint cars. Many talented drivers chose to race Modified Stock cars because they didn't feel comfortable without something over their head. The introduction of roll bars in the 1950s did little to give young upcoming drivers comfort. There had been a lot of resistance to installing roll bars; the opposition to cages was even more intense.

Tom and Richard Holynski, owners of the famous Holynski Brothers shop in Lackawanna, New York, brought a caged Sprint car to Reading for a USAC race in 1964. The brothers built and raced caged Super-Modifieds at Oswego, New York Speedway for a number of years. These types of cars, originally called Eagle class cars, were being raced in the Midwest, primarily in Michigan, before arriving in Oswego in 1961 for the Labor Day race. Because they outran everything else, the caged Super Modifieds were adopted as the featured cars at Oswego starting with the 1962 season opener. In 1966 the speedway changed the name of the cars from Eagle class to Super-Modifieds. The Sprint car the Holynskis brought to Reading featured a chromed cage that was beautifully crafted and integrated into the car chassis. It blended in with the cockpit mostly because of the Holynski's exceptional talent in building attractive and functional racecars. Among the drivers who drove the red Holynski Special were Jim Hurtibuise and Bobby Marshman. The Holynski's cage didn't catch on.

The Holynski's father Walter got the family started in racing. The two sons owned Franklin Motors in Lackawanna. Starting out as a gas station, the business grew into a new car dealership, selling first Nash and Ramblers, and then American Motors products including Jeep. Doing all their own work, they built and raced Sprint cars from the mid to late 1950s into the 1960s. By the early 1970s, they were building Super-Modifieds for others to run at Oswego while racing their own two-car team. Eventually they went into racecar restoration.

Sprint car deaths kept mounting. Red Riegel and Jud Larson were killed in a USAC Sprint car race at Reading on June 11, 1966. The following month, on July 16, Ron Lux was killed in a USAC Sprint car race at the Tulsa, Oklahoma Fairgrounds. Lux was the 1965 Super Modified point champion at Oswego Speedway. On November 12, Don Branson died, along with USAC newcomer Dick Atkins, in a Sprint car race at Gardena, California. Branson enjoyed a very successful and productive career and announced earlier that the Gardena race would be his last race before retiring.

Horrible memories of 1955 resurfaced. The wave of drivers' deaths finally sparked the growing sentiment that something needed to be done considering the awesome speed and the aggressive passing that had become commonplace in Sprint car racing.

Riegel and Larson were both friends of Hinnershitz. Larson and Hinnershitz were friends for years. There was a mutual respect there. Jud Larson adored Hinnershitz. Larson, a Texan born January 21, 1923, who adopted Indianapolis as his home, and Riegel, born July 20, 1931, in Leesport, Pennsylvania, were killed when their cars collided on the second lap of a 30-lap feature race. Many different accounts of what happened surfaced. The most popular explanation is that Larson was aiming for a hole in back of Red's car that wasn't there yet, a common move for a driver who wants to win the race. When Riegel had to back off, the hole Larson had planned to go through never materialized. When he hit Riegel's car, the impact sent both machines up the turn's short embankment. The cars bounced back on to the track, ran up the embankment a second time, and came back on the track before flipping over, trapping the drivers inside. Nobody will ever know whether roll cages would have saved their lives. But roll cages would have certainly increased the odds in their favor to survive the accident.

For some reason, Riegel struggled to get rides in decent equipment. That struggle delayed his development into eventually becoming one of the most talented dirt track drivers ever to compete. Most say his talent had not yet peaked. But he was already 34 years old; he had a lot of catching up to do. His fearless, hard charging style would have enabled him to increase the pace, make up for lost time, and go on to greatness. He passed his Indianapolis rookie test the previous month.

In Bruce Homeyer's Konstant Hot Special Midget, Riegel virtually ruled the one-third-mile Hatfield, Pennsylvania oval. But he couldn't get the regular ride in the car. Finally he got a ride in John Wergland's Sprint car and experienced success when Wergland went to USAC. Then he got the job to drive for Louis Seymour, whose car worked the best for him.

Riegel was survived by his widow, Ellen, daughter Colleen, 9, and son Lee, 7. He's buried at Bern Church Cemetery near Bernville, Pennsylvania. Larson left his widow, Ruth, and three daughters: Beverly, 20, Pamela Joyce, 7, and Doris Jean, 1. He's buried at Capital Memorial Park, Pflugerville, Texas.

After the tragedies of 1966, the consensus within the sport still continued to be against cages. Many said putting a cage on a Sprint car was converting it into a stock car. Many thought that if a driver needed a cage over his head, he didn't have the courage necessary to be a Sprint car driver.

During the period covering the late 1960s and early 1970s, more and more racetracks, especially in Central Pennsylvania, converted from their local versions of Super-Modifieds to Sprint cars with cages and wings. These new versions of Sprint cars were being called "Winged Super Sprints." Before long, race fans from other areas were reading about these new style racecars, the "Pennsylvania Posse" in its infancy, with very fast lap times and intense, close competition. URC brainstormed the idea to bolt on cages. If a promoter wanted Super Sprint car racing, URC would compete with cages. For promoters who wanted traditional Sprint cars, the URC members left their cages at home. That lasted for a little while. Most felt the bolt-on cages were not up to safety standards because they were not an integral part of the racecar. They were basically cosmetic.

The case for cages grew until their adoption became inevitable. Finally, the time had arrived to give the drivers the protection they needed to pursue faster speeds and the aggressive driving style that the V8 powered cars now allowed. The time had finally arrived for cages. Although there is no way to guarantee the safety of a racecar driver, cages have prevented countless serious injuries, and saved many lives.

Chapter 17

The Legend Lives On

In the barnstorming years of the 1930s, 1940s, and 1950s, Tommy Hinnershitz set the standards for driving Sprint cars. He became a legend. Many upcoming drivers who wanted to break into and be successful at the championship level competing with AAA and later USAC were advised to study Hinnershitz in detail. They were told to watch how he ran time trials, how he ran a heat race, and of course how he adapted to changing track conditions when competing in the feature event. They knew the master not only won races with pure horsepower and driving skills; he won races because he was a thinker, preparing for a day of racing by bringing to the track a racecar as near to perfect running order as possible with the correct gearing, tires, and weight distribution set-up. Depending on his inspection of the track before warm-ups, Hinnershitz adjusted all these factors after warm-ups and before the heat race, especially when it came to weight distribution and tire stagger, running the right size and type of tires on each of the four corners of the car. He never tried to break track records. He claimed never to consciously go after a track record. He believed that if everything goes well, records will be broken.

He was born to drive, and not just racecars. The first time he ever drove a car, he was 10 years old. Hinnershitz shared in an interview a story about a car salesman bringing a Model T Touring car to the Hinnershitz house so Al could take it for a test drive. After the drive, Al and the salesman went into the house evidently to discuss a deal to buy the car. Ten-year-old Tommy Hinnershitz decided he needed to also test drive the car, so he drove it around the block. The young boy, already a daredevil, didn't sit too well for a while.

Many consider Hinnershitz's contribution to Sprint car racing comparable to Babe Ruth's to baseball. A. J. Foyt , who has been quoted saying Hinnershitz was the best dirt track Sprint car driver that ever lived, told of how the fans booed him when he came east and started breaking Hinnershitz's records. Other drivers talked of being concerned with the wrath of fans in the pits after beating him. Hinnershitz and Foyt became good friends, and there was mutual admiration. Hinnershitz believed that A. J. Foyt is the greatest racecar driver of all time. It's hard to argue with his professional opinion. Foyt has won just about everything that can be won in auto-racing.

Hinnershitz didn't consider himself more talented than other drivers; he just thought he worked harder. During the week, serving as his own chief mechanic, he worked on his racecar in his garage between 50 and 60 hours per week for most of the year. He was modest and independent minded. When he was a young man, he taught himself to meet a challenge head on and do whatever needed to be done right the first time, not to have to go back and do it again. His engineering skills were as legendary as his racing talent. When he started driving and owning his own cars, he welcomed the fact he didn't have to ask an owner or mechanic for permission to make changes to the car. He learned to think out solutions to problems and make everything work the way he felt most comfortable. On the weekends at the races, he wore his driver's suit of bluish, gray coveralls and a pair of cheap work gloves to protect his hands. In the pits, he usually wore a big farmer's straw hat to keep the hot, blazing sun off his head.

He received the nickname "The Flying Dutchman" for his ability to turn extremely fast times, even with the most terrible track conditions. While meeting these common challenges at the dirt tracks where he mostly raced, his skills were unmatched. During the powerful slides he performed on those loose dirt track turns before the advent of clay; the knobby tires created large "rooster tails" of dirt while he seemed to be able to gain speed instead of losing it. The power slides up high on the outside became his signature move, the Hinnershitz style of dirt track racing.

After a career honorably representing his state, Hinnershitz was inducted into the Pennsylvania Sports Hall of Fame. Later he was inducted into the National Sprint Car Hall of Fame. He was a charter member of the Indianapolis Drivers Association. He was most proud of being named Berks County, Pennsylvania Athlete of the Year for 1952.

He said in an interview his worst racing memory was witnessing the horrendous crash that killed his friends Riegel and Larson in 1966 at Reading. His fondest memory was "Tommy Hinnershitz Day" in 1955 at the Reading Fairgrounds when fans and the track management bestowed him with gifts, including a brand new car.

Hinnershitz's last Midwest win came at New Bremen, Ohio, on September 6, 1959, and his last victory close to home came on October 11, 1959, at Williams Grove. His last race was September 24, 1960, in Allentown, the day his friend Johnny Thomson lost his life.

The headline the next day on the front page of the Sunday morning edition of the *Reading Eagle*, as well as coverage in many other newspapers, announced Thomson's death and Hinnershitz's retirement. While racing fans mourned the death of Thomson, most seemed to breathe a sigh of relief when told of Hinnershitz's retirement. He would now become a living legend, not a dead one like so many of his contemporaries. Walking away unscathed and alive after being exposed to danger all those years was his biggest win.

Hinnershitz lived a busy life, even in his later years, surviving a near tragic farm accident. Despite having two heart attacks during the 1970s, he continued to live independently after the death of Betty in 1993.

He was found dead on the afternoon of August 1, 1999, at

his house. He was 87 and likely died of natural causes. His two daughters, Jeanne and Carol, five grandchildren, eight great-grandchildren, and his sister Kathryn survived him.

He was buried next to Betty in the Spies's Church Cemetery located two miles from his farm and five miles from the shopping center built over top of the dirt that captivated him so early in his life, the Reading Fairgrounds' half-mile oval.

Career Statistics

Tommy Hinnershitz

KEY: DNS: *Did Not Start* DNF: *Did Not Finish* DNQ: *Did Not Qualify* DNP: *Did Not Place* DPO: *Dropped Out*

During a 32-year career competing as a national championship race car driver beginning in 1928, Tommy Hinnershitz specialized in racing Sprint cars on 1/2-mile dirt racetracks.

He was Eastern AAA (American Automobile Association) Sprint car champion 5 times, Eastern USAC (United States Auto Club) Sprint car champion 2 times, and runner-up for the AAA title 4 times. His career statistics include 103 Sprint car victories, 93 Sprint car 2nd-place finishes, and 57 Sprint car 3rd-place finishes. He won 7 Midget car races and finished in the top 10 in Championship car races 14 times. He competed 3 times in the Indianapolis 500, finishing 32nd in 1940, 10th in 1941, and 9th in 1948.

He held 39 track records at the time of his retirement in 1960 and scored more points in Sprint car competition than any other driver in the history of AAA.

His top-place finishes came during an era when Sprint cars typically competed in just one race per week, mostly on state and county fair horse tracks throughout the country.

He was inducted into the Pennsylvania Sports Hall of Fame in

1975 and the National Sprint Car Hall of Fame in its first class in 1990. He was also inducted into the Eastern Museum of Motor Racing in Mechanicsburg, Pennsylvania, and the York County Racing Club Hall of Fame in York, Pennsylvania. His most treasured award, however, was receiving the 1952 Top Athlete Award from the Berks County, Pennsylvania Chamber of Commerce. He was a charter member of the Indianapolis Drivers Association.

During his long career, Hinnershitz drove many different racecars. His standout rides included his own bluebirds and Miracle Power Specials and the Pfrommer Offy, owned by John Pfrommer. The most memorable car owners he drove for included John Gerber, Mark Light, Ted Horn, Dutch Culp, Sex Periman, Buster Warke, Gus Strupp, Jules Furslew, Dr. Raymond Sabourin, Louis Kimmel, Joe Marks, Milt Marion, and Ed Walsh.

1928

September 15, 1928
Reading, PA. Reading Fairgrounds. 1/2-mile dirt. Special Model T event: finished 5th.

1931

September 19, 1931
Reading, PA. Reading Fairgrounds. 1/2-mile dirt. Special Model T event: finished 3rd.

1933

October 1, 1933
Hughesville, PA. Lycoming County Fairgrounds. 1/2-mile dirt. Sprint car event. 10-lap consolation: finished 2nd.

1934

Final Standings:
Finished 63rd in Hankinson Sprint car standings with 80 points.

April 29, 1934
Schuylkill Haven, PA. Cressona Fairgrounds. 1/2-mile dirt. Sprint car event. 10-lap consolation: finished 2nd.

May 20, 1934
Reading, PA. Reading Fairgrounds. 1/2-mile dirt. Sprint car event. 10-lap consolation: DPO. *Hinnershitz scraped the guardrail in the first turn. He tried to get the car straightened out but hit the fence while entering the backstretch.*

July 22, 1934
Hohokus, NJ. 1/2-mile dirt. Sprint car event. 10-lap consolation: DPO.

August 11, 1934
Langhorne, PA. 1-mile dirt. Sprint car event. Time trial: 46:10 seconds. DNS.

September 1, 1934
Flemington, NJ. Flemington Fairgrounds. 1/2-mile dirt. Sprint car event. 10-lap consolation: finished 1st.

September 3, 1934
Flemington, NJ. Flemington Fairgrounds. 1/2-mile dirt. Sprint car event. 10-lap consolation: finished 5th.

September 9, 1934
Hokokus, NJ. 1/2-mile dirt. Sprint car event. 10-lap consolation: finished 5th.

1935

Final Standings:
Finished 13th in Eastern AAA Sprint car standings with 361 points; finished 10th in Hankinson Sprint car standings with 905 points; finished 16th in Central Pennsylvania Sprint car standings with 73 points.

April 13, 1935
Lebanon, PA. Lebanon Fairgrounds. 1/2-mile dirt. Sprint car event. Time trial: 31.00 seconds. 5-lap dash: finished 1st. 10-lap heat: finished 1st. 15-lap feature: finished 1st.

April 21, 1935
Lebanon, PA. Lebanon Fairgrounds. 1/2-mile dirt. Sprint car event. 10-lap heat: finished 2nd. 25-lap feature: finished 2nd.

April 28, 1935
Reading, PA. Reading Fairgrounds. 1/2-mile dirt. Sprint car event. Time trial: 30.45 seconds.
Hinnershitz replaced Ray Shollenberger in Herm Kauffman's car. During the consolation, he crashed through the 3rd turn fence when an axle broke. The car came to a stop inside a Reading Fairgrounds horse barn. He was uninjured.

May 4, 1935
Lebanon, PA. Lebanon Fairgrounds. 1/2-mile dirt. Sprint car event. Time trial: 30.00 seconds. 10-lap heat: finished 2nd. 25-lap feature: DNF.

May 12, 1935
Langhorne, PA. 1-mile dirt. Sprint car event. 10-lap consolation: finished 4th.

May 19, 1935
Lehighton, PA. Lehighton Fairgrounds. 1/2-mile dirt. Sprint car event. 10-lap heat: finished 3rd. 30-lap feature: DNP.

May 30, 1935
Lehighton, PA. Lehighton Fairgrounds. 1/2-mile dirt. Sprint car event. 10-lap heat: finished 3rd. 30-lap feature: DNP.

June 16, 1935
Langhorne, PA. 1-mile dirt. Sprint car event. 10-mile consolation: finished 4th. 50-mile feature: DNP.

June 30, 1935
Woodbridge, NJ. 1/2-mile dirt. Sprint car event. 10-lap heat: finished 1st. 40-lap feature: DNP.

July 3, 1935
Woodbridge, NJ. 1/2-mile dirt. Sprint car event. 10 lap heat: finished 1st. 40-lap feature: DNP.

July 4, 1935
Schuylkill Haven, PA. Cressona Fairgrounds. 1/2-mile dirt. Sprint car event. 15-lap consolation: finished 2nd.

July 11, 1935
Woodbridge, NJ. 1/2-mile dirt. Sprint car event. 10-lap consolation: finished 1st. 40-lap feature: DNP.

July 14, 1935
Hohokus, NJ. 1/2-mile dirt. Sprint car event. 10-lap heat: finished 3rd. 30-lap feature: DNP.

July 18, 1935
Woodbridge, NJ. 1/2-mile dirt. Sprint car event. 10-lap consolation: finished 3rd.

July 21, 1935
Bird-in-Hand, PA. Central Speedway. 1/2-mile dirt. Sprint car event. Time trial: 29.00 seconds. 10-lap heat: finished 1st. 25-lap feature: finished 2nd.

August 8, 1935
Woodbridge, NJ. 1/2-mile dirt. Sprint car event. 10-lap consolation: finished 5th.

August 10, 1935
Lewistown, PA. Lewistown Fairgrounds. 1/2-mile dirt. Sprint car event. 10-lap heat: finished 1st. 30-lap feature: finished 4th.

August 15, 1935
Woodbridge, NJ. 1/2-mile dirt. Sprint car event. 10-lap consolation: finished 3rd.

August 17, 1935
Afton, NY. 1/2-mile dirt. Sprint car event. 10-lap heat: finished 1st. 25-lap feature: DNP.

August 18, 1935
Lehighton, PA. Lehighton Fairgrounds. 1/2-mile dirt. Sprint car event. Time trial: 28.50 seconds. 10-lap heat: finished 2nd. 30-lap feature: finished 2nd.

August 22, 1935
Woodbridge, NJ. 1/2-mile dirt. Sprint car event. 10-lap heat: finished 3rd. 40-lap feature: finished 7th.

August 30, 1935
Woodbridge, NJ. 1/2-mile dirt. Sprint car event. 10-lap heat: finished 2nd. 40-lap feature: finished 5th.

August 31, 1935
Flemington, NJ. Flemington Fairgrounds. 1/2-mile dirt. Sprint car event. 10-lap heat: finished 2nd. 30-lap feature: finished 2nd.

September 15, 1935
Reading, PA. Reading Fairgrounds. 1/2-mile dirt. Sprint car event. 10-lap consolation: finished 2nd.

September 21, 1935
Allentown, PA. Allentown Fairgrounds. 1/2-mile dirt. Sprint car event. 10-lap heat: finished 3rd. 30-lap feature: finished 5th.

September 22, 1935
Hohokus, NJ. 1/2-mile dirt. Sprint car event. 10-lap heat: finished 5th. 10-lap consolation: finished 1st. 30-lap feature: finished 6th.

September 28, 1935
Bloomsburg, PA. Bloomsburg Fairgrounds. 1/2-mile dirt. Sprint car event. Rained out.

September 29, 1935
Trenton, NJ. New Jersey State Fairgrounds. 1/2-mile dirt. Sprint car event. 10-lap heat: finished 1st. 30-lap feature: finished 3rd.

September 30, 1935
Bloomsburg, PA. Bloomsburg Fairgrounds. 1/2-mile dirt. Sprint car event. *During his time trial, Hinnershitz hit the guardrail. The force bent the steering on the Mark Light owned car.* DNS.

October 3, 1935
Atlanta, GA. Lakewood Park. 1-mile dirt. Sprint car event. 5-lap heat: finished 3rd. 25-lap feature: DNF.

1936

Final Standings:
Finished 2nd in Eastern AAA Sprint car standings with 902 points; finished 4th in Hankinson Sprint car standings with 1,470 points; finished 34th in Madison Square Garden Bowl (in Long Island City, New York) standings with 23 points.

April 26, 1936
Reading, PA. Reading Fairgrounds. 1/2-mile dirt. Sprint car event.
Time trial: 28.20 seconds. 10-lap heat: finished 1st. 40-lap feature:
finished 4th.

May 3, 1936
Hohokus, NJ. 1/2-mile dirt. Sprint car event. 10-lap heat: finished
1st. 30-lap feature: finished 3rd.

May 15, 1936
Union, NJ. 1/2-mile dirt. Sprint car event. Time trial: 29.80 seconds.
10-lap heat: finished 2nd. 30-lap feature: finished 4th.

May 17, 1936
Langhorne, PA. 1-mile dirt. Sprint car event. 10-mile heat: DPO.
10-mile consolation: finished 1st. 50-mile feature: DPO after 21 laps
while leading.

May 22, 1936
Union, NJ. 1/2-mile dirt. Sprint car event. Time trial: 29.80 seconds.
10-lap heat: finished 3rd. 30-lap feature: finished 1st.

May 29, 1936
Union, NJ. 1/2-mile dirt. Sprint car event. 10-lap heat: finished 2nd.
30-lap feature: finished 2nd.

May 31, 1936
Hohokus, NJ. 1/2-mile dirt. Sprint car event. 10-lap heat: finished
1st. 40-lap feature: finished 2nd.

June 5, 1936
Union, NJ. 1/2-mile dirt. Sprint car event. Time trial: 29.40 seconds.
10-lap heat: finished 1st. 20-lap feature: finished 1st.

June 21, 1936
Langhorne, PA. 1-mile dirt. Sprint car event. Time trial: 37.00 seconds. 10-mile heat: finished 1st. 100-mile feature: DPO. *Hinnershitz made a total of four pit stops. He was leading when he made his 2nd stop at 32 laps and dropped out on the 78th lap after making his 4th stop.*

June 26, 1936
Union, NJ. 1/2-mile dirt. Sprint car event. 10-lap heat: finished 1st. 30-lap feature: finished 3rd.

June 28, 1936
Hohokus, NJ. 1/2-mile dirt. Sprint car event. Time trial: 29.50 seconds. 10-lap heat: finished 1st. 30-lap feature: finished 1st.

July 4, 1936
Hohokus, NJ. 1/2-mile dirt. Sprint car event. Time trial: 30.20 seconds. 5-lap dash: finished 2nd. 10-lap heat: DPO.

July 10, 1936
Union, NJ. 1/2-mile dirt. Sprint car event. Time trial: 30.20 seconds. 10-lap heat: finished 1st. 30-lap feature: finished 2nd.

July 12, 1936
Reading, PA. Reading Fairgrounds. 1/2-mile dirt. Sprint car event. Time trial: 30.00 seconds. 10-lap heat: finished 3rd. 30-lap feature: finished 4th.

July 18, 1936
Mineola, L.I., NY. Nassau County Fairgrounds. 1/2-mile dirt. Sprint car event. DNF. *Crashed during 3rd heat after hitting Ted Horn and Ray Pixley's stalled cars. There were no injuries, but the cars were heavily damaged.*

July 19, 1936
Hohokus, NJ. 1/2-mile dirt. Sprint car event. 10-lap heat: finished 1st. 30-lap feature: DPO on 16th lap.

July 30, 1936
Union, NJ. 1/2-mile dirt. Sprint car event. 10-lap heat: finished 3rd.
30-lap feature: finished 2nd.

August 8, 1936
Lewistown, PA. Lewistown Fairgrounds. 1/2-mile dirt. Sprint car
event. 10-lap heat: finished 3rd. 30-lap feature: finished 3rd.

August 20, 1936
Union, NJ. 1/2-mile dirt. Sprint car event. 10-lap heat: finished 1st.
30-lap feature: DPO on 5th lap.

August 22, 1936
Middletown, NY. Orange County Fairgrounds. 1/2-mile dirt.
Sprint car event. 10-lap heat: finished 3rd. 30-lap feature: fin-
ished 4th

September 3, 1936
Union, NJ. 1/2-mile dirt. Sprint car event. 10-lap heat: finished 1st.
30-lap feature: finished 1st.

September 9, 1936
Long Island City, NY. Madison Square Garden Bowl. 1/5-mile paved.
Midget car event. 12-lap handicap: finished 5th. 15-lap consolation:
finished 1st. 15-lap consolation: finished 1st. 25-lap feature: DPO.

September 13, 1936
Union, NJ. 1/2-mile dirt. Sprint car event. 10-lap heat: finished 1st.
30-lap feature: finished 1st.

September 19, 1936
Brockton, MA. 1/2-mile dirt. Sprint car event. 10-lap heat: finished
2nd. 30-lap feature: finished 4th.

September 20, 1936
Reading, PA. Reading Fairgrounds. 1/2-mile dirt. Sprint car event.
Time trial: 29.20 seconds. 10-lap heat: finished 4th. 10-lap heat: fin-
ished 1st. 30-lap feature: DPO.

September 26, 1936
Allentown, PA. Allentown Fairgrounds. 1/2-mile dirt. Sprint car event. Time trial: 28.60 seconds. 10-lap heat: finished 1st. 30-lap feature: DPO.

October 2, 1936
Trenton, NJ. New Jersey State Fairgrounds. 1/2-mile dirt. Sprint car event. 30-lap feature: finished 2nd.

October 3, 1936
Bloomsburg, PA. Bloomsburg Fairgrounds. 1/2-mile dirt. Sprint car event. 30-lap feature: finished 3rd.

October 18, 1936
Hohokus, NJ. 1/2-mile dirt. Sprint car event. 10-lap heat: finished 1st. 30-lap feature: finished 1st.

October 24, 1936
Danbury, CT. Danbury Fairgrounds. 1/2-mile dirt. Sprint car event. DNF. *Lost wheel and flipped. Received leg injury.*

1937

Final Standings:
Finished 9th in Eastern AAA Sprint car standings with 335 points; finished 9th in Hankinson Sprint car standings with 1,037 points; finished 18th in Midwest AAA Sprint car standings with 96 points; finished 15th in Eastern NMARA (National Midget Auto Racing Association) Midget car standings with 651 points; finished 14th in Heiserman Midget car standings with 1,340 points.

April 25, 1937
Reading, PA. Reading Fairgrounds. 1/2-mile dirt. Sprint car event. Time trial: 28.30 seconds. 10-lap heat: finished 3rd. 40-lap feature: *car was driven in the feature by Roy Lake.*

May 9, 1937
Union, NJ. 1/2-mile dirt. Sprint car event. Time trial: 30.10 seconds. 10-lap consolation: finished 1st. 30-lap feature: DPO.

May 16, 1937
Langhorne, PA. 1-mile dirt. Sprint car event. 10-mile heat: finished 4th. 10-mile heat: finished 2nd. 50-mile feature: DPO after 16 miles.

May 31, 1937
Hohokus, NJ. 1/2-mile dirt. Sprint car event. 10-lap consolation: finished 2nd.

June 15, 1937
Reading, PA. Lauer's Park. 1/5-mile dirt. Midget car event. 10-lap heat: finished 3rd. 12-lap handicap: finished 1st. 20-lap feature: finished 3rd.

June 18, 1937
Freeport, L.I., NY. Freeport Stadium. 1/5-mile dirt. Midget car event. 10-lap heat: finished 2nd. 15-lap semi: finished 1st. 25-lap feature: DNP.

June 19, 1937
Langhorne, PA. 1-mile dirt. Sprint car event. 10-mile heat: finished 3rd. 50-lap feature: finished 5th.

June 20, 1937
Hohokus, NJ. 1/2-mile dirt. Sprint car event. 10-lap consolation: finished 1st. 30-lap feature: finished 8th.

June 22, 1937
Freeport, L.I., NY. Freeport Stadium. 1/5-mile dirt. Midget car event. 10-lap heat: finished 3rd.

June 24, 1937
Union, NJ. 1/2-mile dirt. Sprint car event. 10-lap heat: finished 1st. 30-lap feature: finished 5th.

June 25, 1937
Long Branch, NJ. 1/5-mile dirt. Midget car event. 10-lap heat: finished 3rd.

June 29, 1937
Freeport, L.I., NY. Freeport Stadium. 1/5-mile dirt. Midget car event. 10-lap heat: finished 4th. 15-lap semi: finished 3rd. 25-lap feature: finished 3rd.

July 4, 1937
Hohokus, NJ. 1/2-mile dirt. Sprint car event. 10-lap heat: finished 3rd. 30-lap feature: finished 6th.

July 5, 1937
Altamont, NY. 1/2-mile dirt. Sprint car event. 30-lap feature: finished 3rd.

July 11, 1937
Cedar Rapids, IA. Frontier Park. 1/2-mile dirt. Sprint car event. 10-lap heat: finished 3rd. 30-lap feature: DNP.

July 18, 1937
Chicago, IL. Cook County Fairgrounds. 1/2-mile dirt. Sprint car event. 10-lap heat: finished 3rd. 12-lap handicap: finished 1st. 50-lap feature: finished 3rd.

July 21, 1937
Camden, NJ. Airport Speedway. 1/5-mile dirt. Midget car event. 10-lap heat: finished 1st. 12-lap handicap: finished 3rd. 20-lap feature: DNF. *Spun out.*

July 29, 1937
Savin Rock, CT. Donovan Field. 1/5-mile dirt. Midget car event. 10-lap heat: finished 1st. 20-lap feature: finished 3rd.

July 30, 1937
Freeport, L.I., NY. Freeport Stadium. 1/5-mile dirt. Midget car event. 10-lap heat: finished 3rd. 12-lap semi: finished 3rd. 25-lap feature: DNP.

August 1, 1937
Chicago, IL. Cook County Fairgrounds. 1/2-mile dirt. Sprint car event. 10-lap heat: DPO.

August 3, 1937
Freeport, L.I., NY. Freeport Stadium. 1/5-mile dirt. Midget car event. 10-lap heat: finished 4th. 12-lap semi: finished 5th. 25-lap feature: finished 2nd.

August 5, 1937
Savin Rock, CT. Donovan Field. 1/5-mile dirt. Midget car event. 10-lap heat: finished 3rd.

August 6, 1937
Freeport, L.I., NY. Freeport Stadium. 1/5-mile dirt. Midget car event. 10-lap heat: finished 4th. 15-lap semi: finished 1st. 25-lap feature: finished 2nd.

August 8, 1937
Hohokus, NJ. 1/2-mile dirt. Sprint car event. 10-lap heat: DPO.

August 10, 1937
Freeport, L.I., NY. Freeport Stadium. 1/5-mile dirt. Midget car event. 10-lap heat: finished 4th. 15-lap semi: finished 1st. 25-lap feature: finished 3rd.

August 11, 1937
Long Beach, NJ. 1/5-mile dirt. Midget car event. 10-lap heat: finished 2nd. 12-lap handicap: finished 1st. 20-lap feature: finished 2nd.

August 13, 1937
Freeport, L.I., NY. Freeport Stadium. 1/5-mile dirt. Midget car event. 10-lap heat: finished 4th. 15-lap semi: finished 2nd. 25-lap main event: DNP.

August 16, 1937
Philadelphia, PA. Yellow Jacket Speedway. 1/5-mile dirt. Midget car event. 10-lap heat: finished 2nd. 20-lap feature: DNF. *Spun out.*

August 17, 1937
Freeport, L.I., NY. Freeport Stadium. 1/5-mile dirt. Midget car event. 10-lap heat: finished 3rd. 15-lap semi: finished 5th. 25-lap feature: DNP.

August 18, 1937
Long Branch, NJ. 1/5-mile dirt. Midget car event. 10-lap heat: finished 2nd. 20-lap feature: finished 2nd.

August 21, 1937
Springfield, IL. Illinois State Fairgrounds. 1-mile dirt. Sprint car event. Time trial: 42.18 seconds. 100-mile feature: DPO.

August 22, 1937
Milwaukee, WI. Wisconsin State Fairgrounds. 1-mile dirt. Sprint car event. 10-mile heat: finished 3rd. 25-mile feature: DNP.

August 23, 1937
Philadelphia, PA. Yellow Jacket Speedway. 1/5-mile dirt. Midget car event. 10-lap heat: finished 2nd. 30-lap feature: finished 1st.

August 26, 1937
Milwaukee, WI. Wisconsin State Fairgrounds. 1-mile dirt. Sprint car event. DNS. *Mechanical problems.*

August 31, 1937
Freeport, L.I., NY. Freeport Stadium. 1/5-mile dirt. Midget car event. 10-lap heat: finished 3rd.

September 3, 1937
Freeport, L.I., NY. Freeport Stadium. 1/5-mile dirt. Midget car event. 10-lap heat: finished 3rd. 15-lap semi: finished 2nd. 25-lap feature: finished 4th.

September 6, 1937
Flemington, NJ. Flemington Fairgrounds. 1/2-mile dirt. Sprint car event. 10-lap heat: finished 3rd. 30-lap feature: DNP.

September 6, 1937
Philadelphia, PA. Yellow Jacket Speedway. 1/5-mile dirt. Midget car event. 10-lap consolation: finished 1st. 15-lap handicap: finished 2nd.

September 10, 1937
Freeport, L.I., NY. Freeport Stadium. 1/5-mile dirt. Midget car event. 10-lap heat: finished 2nd. 12-lap consolation: finished 2nd.

September 11, 1937
Rutland, VT. 1/2-mile dirt. Sprint car event. 10-lap heat: finished 3rd. 30-lap feature: DPO.

September 12, 1937
Schuylkill Haven, PA. Cressona Fairgrounds. 1/2-mile dirt. Sprint car event. Time trial: 27.40 seconds. 10-lap heat: finished 1st. 30-lap feature: DPO.

September 19, 1937
Chicago, IL. Cook County Fairgrounds. 1/2-mile dirt. Sprint car event. DNS. *Mechanical problems.*

September 24, 1937
Clearfield, PA. Clearfield Fairgrounds. 1/2-mile dirt. Sprint car event. DNS. *Crashed and received minor injuries.*

October 4, 1937
Philadelphia, PA. Yellow Jacket Speedway. 1/5-mile dirt. Midget car event. 10-lap heat: finished 1st.

October 5, 1937
Freeport, L.I., NY. Freeport Stadium. 1/5-mile dirt. Midget car event. 10-lap heat: finished 1st. 12-lap semi: finished 4th. 25-lap feature: DNS. *Rained out.*

October 8, 1937
Freeport, L.I., NY. Freeport Stadium. 1/5-mile dirt. Midget car event. 10-lap heat: finished 5th. 12-lap semi: finished 1st. 25-lap feature: finished 4th.

October 9, 1937
Savin Rock, CT. Donovan Field. 1/5-mile dirt. Midget car event. 15-lap consolation: finished 1st.

October 11, 1937
Philadelphia, PA. Yellow Jacket Speedway. 1/5-mile dirt. Midget car event. 100-lap feature: finished 3rd.

October 12, 1937
Freeport, L.I., NY. Freeport Stadium. 1/5-mile dirt. Midget car event. 100-lap feature: finished 3rd.

October 16, 1937
Raleigh, NC. 1/2-mile dirt. Sprint car event. 25-lap feature: finished 2nd.

October 17, 1937
Union, NJ. 1/2-mile dirt. Sprint car event. 10-lap heat: finished 1st. 30-lap feature: finished 1st.

October 18, 1937
Raleigh, NC. 1/2-mile event. Sprint car event. 25-lap feature: finished 2nd.

October 28, 1937
Wilmington, NC. 1/2-mile dirt. Sprint car event. 10-lap heat: DPO.

November 17, 1937
Ft. Worth, TX. Will Rogers Coliseum. 1/8-mile dirt. Midget car event. 10-lap heat: finished 5th. 25-lap feature: finished 5th.

November 21, 1937
Houston, TX. Speed Bowl. 1/5-mile dirt. Midget car event. 10-lap heat: finished 3rd. 12-lap semi: finished 5th. 25-lap feature: finished 9th.

November 24, 1937
Ft. Worth, TX. Will Rogers Coliseum. 1/8-mile dirt. Midget car event. 10-lap heat: finished 1st. 25-lap feature: finished 6th.

November 25, 1937
Houston, TX. Speed Bowl. 1/5-mile dirt. Midget car event. 10-lap heat: finished 3rd. 12-lap semi: finished 6th. 15-lap consolation: finished 4th.

November 26, 1937
Houston, TX. Speed Bowl. 1/5-mile dirt. Midget car event. 10-lap heat: finished 3rd. 25-lap feature: finished 7th.

1938

Final Standings:
Finished 2nd in Eastern AAA Sprint car standings with 380 points; finished 36th in Central Pennsylvania Sprint car standings with 10 points; finished 19th in AAA National Championship car standings with 45 points; finished 5th in Eastern AAA Midget car standings with 1,137 points.

April 3, 1938
Nutley, NJ. Velodrome. 1/7-mile high-banked board. Midget car event. 10-lap heat: finished 2nd. 15-lap semi: finished 2nd. 35-lap feature: finished 4th.

April 24, 1938
Reading, PA. Reading Fairgrounds. 1/2-mile dirt. Sprint car event. Time trial: 26.50 seconds. 10-lap heat: finished 1st. 40-lap feature: DPO while leading.

May 1, 1938
Hohokus, NJ. 1/2-mile dirt. Sprint car event. 30-lap feature: DPO. *Day race. Ran that night at Nutley, NJ.*

May 1, 1938
Nutley, NJ. Velodrome. 1/7-mile high-banked board. Midget car event. 10-lap heat: DPO.

May 4, 1938
Nutley, NJ. Velodrome. 1/7-mile high-banked board. Midget car event. DNS. *Mechanical problems.*

May 8, 1938
Nutley, NJ. Velodrome. 1/7-mile high-banked board. Midget car event. 15-lap consolation: finished 1st.

May 11, 1938
Nutley, NJ. Velodrome. 1/7-mile high-banked board. Midget car event. 10-lap heat: finished 3rd. 15-lap semi: finished 3rd. 35-lap feature: finished 5th.

May 22, 1938
Nutley, NJ. Velodrome. 1/7-mile high-banked board. Midget car event. 10-lap heat: finished 3rd.

May 25, 1938
Nutley, NJ. Velodrome. 1/7-mile high-banked board. Midget car event. 10-lap heat: finished 2nd. 15-lap consolation: DPO. *Hit guard rail while running 3rd.*

May 29, 1938
Hohokus, NJ. 1/2-mile dirt. Sprint car event. 30-lap feature: finished 3rd. *Replaced Gus Zarka. Day race. Ran that night at Nutley, NJ.*

May 29, 1938
Nutley, NJ. Velodrome. 1/7-mile high-banked board. Midget car event. 10-lap heat: finished 2nd. 35-lap feature: finished 3rd.

June 1, 1938
Nutley, NJ. Velodrome. 1/7-mile high-banked board. Midget car event. 10-lap heat: finished 2nd. 15-lap semi: finished 3rd. 35-lap feature: finished 4th.

June 2, 1938
Cedarhurst, L.I., NY. 1/4-mile paved. Midget car event. 8-lap heat: finished 3rd. 8-lap handicap: finished 3rd.

June 7, 1938
Philadelphia, PA. Yellow Jacket Speedway. 1/5-mile dirt. Midget car event. 10-lap heat: finished 1st. 10-lap handicap: finished 2nd. 15-lap semi: finished 2nd. 25-lap feature: finished 2nd.

June 8, 1938
Nutley, NJ. Velodrome. 1/7-mile high-banked board. Midget car event. 10-lap heat: finished 2nd. 15-lap semi: finished 1st. 35-lap feature: DPO after 3 laps.

June 9, 1938
Cedarhurst, L.I., NY. 1/4-mile paved. Midget car event. 8-lap heat: finished 3rd. 8-lap handicap: finished 3rd. 25-lap feature: DNP.

June 10, 1938
Philadelphia, PA. Yellow Jacket Speedway. 1/5-mile dirt. Midget car event. 10-lap heat: finished 2nd. 10-lap handicap: finished 2nd.

June 13, 1938
Bridgeport, CT. Newfield Park. 1/5-mile dirt. Midget car event. 10-lap heat: finished 1st.

June 19, 1938
Nutley, NJ. Velodrome. 1/7-mile high-banked board. Midget car event. 10-lap heat: finished 2nd. 15-lap semi: finished 1st. 35-lap feature: finished 1st.

June 20, 1938
Bridgeport, CT. Newfield Park. 1/5-mile dirt. Midget car event. 10-lap heat: finished 1st.

June 21, 1938
Philadelphia, PA. Yellow Jacket Speedway. 1/5-mile dirt. Midget car event. 10-lap heat: finished 2nd. 10-lap handicap: finished 2nd. 15-lap semi: finished 2nd. 25-lap feature: finished 2nd.

June 22, 1938
Nutley, NJ. Velodrome. 1/7-mile high-banked board. Midget car event. 10-lap heat: finished 2nd. 15-lap semi: finished 3rd. 35-lap feature: DPO after 14 laps.

June 23, 1938
Cedarhurst, L.I., NY. 1/4-mile paved. Midget car event. 8-lap heat: finished 2nd. 8-lap handicap: finished 1st.

June 29, 1938
Nutley, NJ. Velodrome. 1/7-mile high-banked board. Midget car event. 10-lap heat: finished 3rd. 15-lap semi: DPO

July 3, 1938
Nutley, NJ. Velodrome. 1/7-mile high-banked board. Midget car event. 10-lap heat: finished 3rd. 15-lap semi: finished 2nd. 35-lap feature: finished 2nd.

July 4, 1938
Hobokus, NJ. 1/2-mile dirt. Sprint car event. 10-lap heat: finished 2nd.

July 6, 1938
Nutley, NJ. Velodrome. 1/7-mile high-banked board. Midget car event. 10-lap heat: finished 4th. 15-lap semi: finished 2nd. 35-lap feature: finished 2nd.

July 8, 1938
Nutley, NJ. Velodrome. 1/7-mile high-banked board. Midget car event. 10-lap heat: finished 1st. 15-lap semi: finished 1st. 35-lap feature: finished 2nd.

July 10, 1938
Nutley, NJ. Velodrome. 1/7-mile high-banked board. Midget car event. 10-lap heat: finished 1st. 15-lap semi: finished 1st. 35-lap feature: finished 2nd.

July 12, 1938
Philadelphia, PA. Yellow Jacket Speedway. 1/5-mile dirt. Midget car event. 12-lap heat: finished 2nd. 50-lap feature: finished 1st.

July 17, 1938
Nutley, NJ. Velodrome. 1/7-mile high-banked board. Midget car event. 10-lap heat: finished 3rd. 15-lap semi: finished 3rd. 35-lap feature: DPO after 28 laps.

July 19, 1938
Philadelphia, PA. Yellow Jacket Speedway. 1/5-mile dirt. Midget car event. DNS. *Mechanical problems.*

July 20, 1938
Nutley, NJ. Velodrome. 1/7-mile high-banked board. Midget car event. DNS. *Mechanical problems.*

July 21, 1938
Cedarhurst, L.I., NY. 1/4-mile paved. Midget car event. 8-lap heat: finished 2nd. 8-lap handicap: finished 3rd. 25-lap feature: finished 3rd.

July 24, 1938
Nutley, NJ. Velodrome. 1/7-mile high-banked board. Midget car event. 10-lap heat: finished 3rd. 15-lap semi: finished 1st. 35-lap feature: DPO on 33rd lap while leading; awarded 5th place.

July 25, 1938
Cedarhurst, L.I., NY. 1/4-mile paved. Midget car event. 8-lap heat: finished 2nd. 25-lap feature: finished 3rd.

July 26, 1938
Philadelphia, PA. Yellow Jacket Speedway. 1/5-mile dirt. Midget car event. 10-lap heat: finished 1st. 10-lap handicap: finished 3rd. 15-lap handicap: finished 4th. 25-lap feature: finished 1st.

July 27, 1938
Nutley, NJ. Velodrome. 1/7-mile high-banked board. Midget car event. 10-lap heat: finished 3rd.

July 28, 1938
Cedarhurst, L.I., NY. 1/4-mile paved. Midget car event. 8-lap heat: finished 3rd. 8-lap handicap: finished 2nd. 25-lap feature: finished 1st.

July 30, 1938
Harrington, DE. Kent-Sussex County Fairgrounds. 1/2-mile dirt. Sprint car event. 10-lap heat: finished 6th. 10-lap heat: finished 5th. 10-lap consolation: finished 1st.

July 31, 1938
Nutley, NJ. Velodrome. 1/7-mile high-banked board. Midget car event. 10-lap heat: finished 3rd. 15-lap semi: finished 4th. 50-lap feature: finished 5th.

August 1, 1938
Cedarhurst, L.I., NY. 1/4-mile paved. Midget car event. 8-lap heat: finished 3rd.

August 2, 1938
Philadelphia, PA. Yellow Jacket Speedway. 1/5-mile dirt. Midget car event. 10-lap heat: finished 1st. 10-lap handicap: finished 1st. 25-lap feature: finished 3rd.

August 8, 1938
Cedarhurst, L.I., NY. 1/4-mile paved. Midget car event. 8-lap heat: finished 3rd.

August 9, 1938
Philadelphia, PA. Yellow Jacket Speedway. 1/5-mile dirt. Midget car event. 10-lap consolation: finished 1st. 75-lap feature: *Paul Russo drove the car in the feature.*

August 10, 1938
Nutley, NJ. Velodrome. 1/7-mile high-banked board. Midget car event. 15-lap semi: finished 1st. 35-lap feature: finished 3rd.

August 14, 1938
Nutley, NJ. Velodrome. 1/7-mile high-banked board. Midget car event. 10-lap heat: finished 3rd. 15-lap semi: finished 1st. 15-lap semi: finished 1st. 35-lap feature: finished 3rd.

August 15, 1938
Cedarhurst, L.I., NY. 1/4-mile paved. Midget car event. 8-lap heat: finished 3rd. 8-lap handicap: finished 3rd. 40-lap feature: finished 4th.

August 16, 1938
Philadelphia, PA. Yellow Jacket Speedway. 1/5-mile dirt. Midget car event. 10-lap heat: finished 3rd. 10-lap handicap: finished 1st. 50-lap feature: finished 3rd.

August 20, 1938
Springfield IL. Illinois State Fairgrounds. 1-mile dirt. Sprint car event. Time trial: 42.01 seconds. 10-mile heat: finished 6th. 100-mile feature: finished 9th.

August 21, 1938
Milwaukee, WI. Wisconsin State Fairgrounds. 1-mile dirt. Sprint car event. Time trial: 44:11 seconds. 5-mile heat: finished 3rd. 25-mile feature: finished 7th.

August 25, 1938
Altamont, NY. 1/2-mile dirt. Sprint car event. 10-lap heat: finished 3rd. 30-lap feature: DPO.

August 26, 1938
Altamont, NY. 1/2-mile dirt. Sprint car event. 10-lap heat: finished 1st. 30-lap feature: finished 2nd.

August 28, 1938
Nutley, NJ. Velodrome. 1/7-mile high-banked board. Midget car event. 10-lap heat: finished 6th. 15-lap consolation: finished 3rd.

August 30, 1938
Philadelphia, PA. Yellow Jacket Speedway. 1/5-mile dirt. Midget car event. 10-lap heat: finished 1st. 10-lap handicap: finished 1st. 15-lap handicap: finished 3rd. 50-lap feature: finished 2nd.

August 31, 1938
Nutley, NJ. Velodrome. 1/7-mile high-banked board. Midget car event. 10-lap heat: finished 2nd. 15-lap semi: finished 3rd. 35-lap feature: finished 5th.

September 3, 1938
Flemington, NJ. Flemington Fairgrounds. 1/2-mile dirt. Sprint car event. 10-lap heat: finished 2nd. 20-lap feature: finished 1st.

September 4, 1938
Nutley, NJ. Velodrome. 1/7-mile high-banked board. Midget car event. 10-lap heat: finished 4th.

September 5, 1938
Altoona, PA. 1 1/8-mile asphalt. Sprint car event. 10-lap heat: finished 4th. 45-lap feature: finished 5th.

September 6, 1938
Philadelphia, PA. Yellow Jacket Speedway. 1/5-mile dirt. Midget car event. 10-lap heat: finished 2nd. 10-lap handicap: finished 1st. 50-lap feature: DNF. *Spun out on 2nd lap.*

September 8, 1938
Cedarhurst, L.I., NY. 1/4-mile paved. Midget car event. 10-lap heat: finished 3rd.

September 10, 1938
Syracuse, NY. New York State Fairgrounds. 1-mile dirt. Championship car event. 100-mile feature: DPO on 67th lap.

September 11, 1938
Schuylkill Haven, PA. Cressona Fairgrounds. 1/2-mile dirt. Sprint car event. 10-lap heat: finished 3rd. 20-lap feature: finished 4th. *Day race. Ran that night at Nutley, NJ.*

September 11, 1938
Nutley, NJ. Velodrome. 1/7-mile high-banked board. Midget car event. 35-lap feature: DPO on 16th lap.

September 24, 1938
Allentown, PA. Allentown Fairgrounds. 1/2-mile dirt. Sprint car event. 10-lap heat: finished 3rd. 30-lap feature: finished 4th.

September 25, 1938
Reading, PA. Reading Fairgrounds. 1/2-mile dirt. Sprint car event. Time trial: 27.50 seconds. 10-lap heat: finished 2nd. 30-lap feature: finished 1st.

September 28, 1938
Nutley, NJ. Velodrome. 1/7-mile high-banked board. Midget car event. 10-lap heat: finished 1st. 15-lap semi: finished 1st. 35-lap feature: *On the 7th lap the racecar's rear wheels locked up. The car slid off the steep banking into the infield and rolled, ending upside down. Hinnershitz escaped serious injury.*

October 1, 1938
Trenton, NJ. New Jersey State Fairgrounds. 1/2-mile dirt. Sprint car event. 10-lap heat: finished 2nd. 30-lap feature: finished 1st.

October 2, 1938
Nutley, NJ. Velodrome. 1/7-mile high-banked board. Midget car event. 10-lap heat: finished 2nd. 15-lap semi: finished 1st. 35-lap feature: finished 3rd.

October 4, 1938
Philadelphia, PA. Yellow Jacket Speedway. 1/5-mile dirt. Midget car event. 10-lap heat: finished 3rd. 150-lap feature: finished 4th. *He led for 120 laps, then had to pit for fuel.*

October 7, 1938
Bronx, NY. Castle Hill Stadium. 1/5-mile dirt. Midget car event. 15-lap semi: finished 1st. 100-lap feature: DNP.

October 8, 1938
Danbury, CT. Danbury Fairgrounds. 1/2-mile dirt. Sprint car event. Time trial: 27.80 seconds. 10-lap heat: finished 2nd. 30-lap feature: finished 2nd.

October 9, 1938
Nutley, NJ. Velodrome. 1/7-mile high-banked board. Midget car event. 15-lap consolation: finished 1st. 35-lap feature: DPO on 17th lap.

October 11, 1938
Philadelphia, PA. Yellow Jacket Speedway. 1/5-mile dirt. Midget car event. 10-lap heat: finished 1st. 15-lap handicap: finished 1st. 50-lap feature: finished 5th.

1939

Final Standings:
Finished 4th in Eastern AAA Sprint car standings with 431 points; finished 4th in the Hankinson Sprint car standings with 1,055 points; finished 31st in Eastern AAA Midget car standings with 861 points; finished 17th in Capitol Speedway, Washington, D.C. standings with 116 points; finished 23rd in Bronx Coliseum (in Bronx, New York) standings with 67 points.

January 8, 1939
Bronx, NY. Bronx Coliseum. 1/6-mile board. Midget car event. 15-lap heat: finished 3rd. 15-lap consolation: finished 1st. 25-lap feature: DNF. *Spun out on 16th lap.*

January 11, 1939
Bronx, NY. Bronx Coliseum. 1/6-mile board. Midget car event. 15-lap consolation: finished 1st. 25-lap feature: finished 3rd.

January 15, 1939
Bronx, NY. Bronx Coliseum. 1/6-mile board. Midget car event. 15-lap heat: finished 1st. 15-lap consolation: finished 1st. 25-lap feature: finished 4th.

January 18, 1939
Bronx, NY. Bronx Coliseum. 1/6-mile board. Midget car event. 15-lap heat: DPO. *Tangled with Bill Morrissey and Bub Walker.*

March 19, 1939
Nutley, NJ. Velodrome. 1/7-mile high-banked board. Midget car event. 12-lap heat: finished 1st. 15-lap semi: finished 3rd. 35-lap feature: DNP.

March 26, 1939
Nutley, NJ. Velodrome. 1/7-mile high-banked board. Midget car event. 15-lap heat: finished 2nd. 15-lap semi: finished 1st. 35-lap feature: DPO after 15 laps.

April 2, 1939
Nutley, NJ. Velodrome. 1/7-mile high-banked board. Midget car event. 15-lap heat: DPO. *Racing down the backstretch with six other cars, Hinnershitz got mixed up with Harry Cassel. Hinnershitz hit the guardrail and was thrown from the car and slid to the track's flat apron. He was taken to the hospital for treatment of minor injuries. He received loud applause from the fans when he returned to the Velodrome. The racecar was badly damaged.*

April 23, 1939
Reading, PA. Reading Fairgrounds. 1/2-mile dirt. Sprint car event. 10-lap heat: finished 2nd. 40-lap feature: finished 2nd.

April 30, 1939
Lebanon, PA. Lebanon Fairgrounds. 1/2-mile dirt. Sprint car event. 10-lap heat: finished 1st. 30-lap feature: finished 4th.

May 14, 1939
Langhorne, PA. 1-mile dirt. Sprint car event. 10-mile heat: finished 3rd. 50-mile feature: finished 2nd.

May 21, 1939
Mechanicsburg, PA. Williams Grove Speedway. 1/2-mile clay.
Sprint car event. 10-lap heat: finished 3rd. 40-lap feature: finished
1st. Time of feature: 19:26.33 minutes. *This was the first race ever
run at Williams Grove Speedway.*

May 24, 1939
Indianapolis, IN. Indianapolis Motor Speedway. 2 1/2-mile brick
and asphalt. Championship car event. Passed rookie test. DNQ.
Drove car owned by Louis Kimmel.

June 4, 1939
Mechanicsburg, PA. Williams Grove Speedway. 1/2-mile clay. Sprint
car event. 10-lap heat: finished 1st. 40-lap feature: finished 5th.

June 5, 1939
Philadelphia, PA. Yellow Jacket Speedway. 1/4-mile paved. Midget
car event. 15-lap handicap: finished 2nd. 40-lap feature: finished
4th.

June 18, 1939
Chicago, IL. Soldier's Field. 1/4-mile banked board track. Midget
car event. 10-lap Class B heat: finished 1st. 35-lap Class B feature:
finished 1st.

June 20, 1939
Chicago, IL. Soldier's Field. 1/4-mile banked board track. Midget
car event. 10-lap Class B heat: finished 1st. 25 lap Class B feature:
finished 1st.

June 23, 1939
Chicago, IL. Soldier's Field. 1/4-mile banked board track. Midget
car event. 10-lap Class B heat: finished 1st. 50-lap Class B feature:
DPO on 48th lap.

July 2, 1939
Mechanicsburg, PA. Williams Grove Speedway. 1/2-mile clay. Sprint car event. 10-lap heat: finished 1st. 40-lap feature: DNF. *On the start, Hinnershitz flipped out over the first turn after tangling with Vic Nauman and Ammon Kelchner. He was uninjured; the car was badly damaged.*

July 5, 1939
Cedarhurst, L.I., NY. 1/4-mile paved. Midget car event. 12-lap heat: finished 2nd. 15-lap semi: finished 1st.

July 7, 1939
Bronx, NY. Castle Hill Stadium. 1/5-mile paved. Midget car event. 15-lap semi: finished 1st. 35-lap feature: finished 2nd.

July 9, 1939
Nutley, NJ. Velodrome. 1/7-mile high-banked board. Midget car event. 15-lap heat: finished 2nd. 15-lap semi: finished 3rd. 25-lap feature: finished 3rd.

July 10, 1939
Philadelphia, PA. Yellow Jacket Speedway. 1/4-mile paved. Midget car event. 40-lap feature: DNF. *Race was red-flagged on the 31st lap when Hinnershitz crashed into the fence and the car rolled over, pinning him underneath. He was uninjured; the car was badly damaged.*

July 12, 1939
Nutley, NJ. Velodrome. 1/7-mile high-banked board. Midget car event. 15-lap heat: finished 1st. 15-lap semi: finished 2nd. 35-lap feature: finished 4th.

July 14, 1939
Bronx, NY. Castle Hill Stadium. 1/5-mile paved. Midget car event. 15-lap heat: finished 2nd.

July 15, 1939
Nutley, NJ. Velodrome. 1/7-mile high-banked board. Midget car event. 15-lap heat: finished 3rd. 15-lap semi: finished 3rd. 35-lap feature: finished 3rd.

July 16, 1939
Mechanicsburg, PA. Williams Grove Speedway. 1/2-mile clay. Sprint car event. 10-lap heat: finished 3rd. 40-lap feature: finished 5th.

July 26, 1939
Nutley, NJ. Velodrome. 1/7-mile high-banked board. Midget car event. 15-lap heat: finished 3rd. 12-lap consolation: finished 1st. 15-lap semi: finished 4th. 35-lap feature: finished 5th.

August 2, 1939
Nutley, NJ. Velodrome. 1/7-mile high-banked board. Midget car event. 15-lap heat: finished 3rd.

August 6, 1939
Lebanon, PA. Lebanon Fairgrounds. 1/2-mile dirt. Sprint car event. 10-lap consolation: finished 1st. 30-lap feature: finished 5th.

August 16, 1939
Nutley, NJ. Velodrome. 1/7-mile high-banked board. Midget car event. 15-lap heat: finished 2nd. 15-lap semi: finished 2nd. 35-lap feature: finished 2nd.

August 19, 1939
Middletown, NY. Orange County Fairgrounds. 1/2-mile dirt. Sprint car event. 10-lap heat: finished 2nd. 30-lap feature: finished 5th.

August 20, 1939
Mechanicsburg, PA. Williams Grove Speedway. 1/2-mile clay. Sprint car event. 10-lap heat: finished 1st. 40-lap feature: finished 1st.

August 22, 1939
Washington, D.C. Capitol Speedway. 1/5-mile paved. Midget car event. 10-lap heat: finished 3rd. 25-lap feature: finished 4th.

August 26, 1939
Hamburg, NY. Erie County Fairgrounds. 1/2-mile dirt. Sprint car event. 10-lap heat: finished 2nd. 30-lap feature: finished 2nd. *Day race. Ran that night at Nutley, NJ.*

August 26, 1939
Nutley, NJ. Velodrome. 1/7-mile high-banked board. Midget car event. 15-lap heat: finished 1st.

August 30, 1939
Washington, D.C. Capitol Speedway. 1/5-mile paved. Midget car event. 15-lap semi: finished 1st. 30-lap feature: DPO on 30th lap.

September 1, 1939
Mechanicsburg, PA. Williams Grove Speedway. 1/2-mile clay. Sprint car event. 12-lap consolation: finished 1st. 40-lap feature: finished 5th.

September 4, 1939
Nutley, NJ. Velodrome. 1/7-mile high-banked board. Midget car event. 15-lap heat: finished 2nd. 15-lap semi: finished 1st. 35-lap feature: DPO on 32nd lap.

September 9, 1939
Washington, D.C. Capitol Speedway. 1/5-mile paved. Midget car event. 10-lap heat: finished 2nd. 12-lap semi: finished 2nd.

September 10, 1939
Altoona, PA. 1 1/8-mile asphalt. Sprint car event. 10-mile heat: finished 3rd. 30-mile feature: DPO.

September 16, 1939
Mineola, LI., NY. Nassau County Fairgrounds. 1/2-mile dirt. Sprint car event. 10-lap heat: finished 1st. 10-lap consolation: finished 1st. 25-lap feature: finished 6th.

September 17, 1939
Reading, PA. Reading Fairgrounds. 1/2-mile dirt. Sprint car event. 10-lap heat: finished 2nd. 30-lap feature: finished 2nd.

September 20, 1939
Baltimore, MD. Municipal Stadium. 1/4-mile dirt. Midget car event. 10-lap heat: finished 2nd.

September 23, 1939
Allentown, PA. Allentown Fairgrounds. 1/2-mile dirt. Sprint car event. 10-lap heat: finished 3rd.

September 24, 1939
Mechanicsburg, PA. Williams Grove Speedway. 1/2-mile clay. Sprint car event. 10-lap heat: finished 1st. 40-lap feature: finished 4th.

September 26, 1939
Washington, D.C. Capitol Speedway. 1/5-mile paved. Midget car event. 10-lap heat: finished 1st. 12-lap semi: finished 2nd.

September 30, 1939
Bloomsburg, PA. Columbia County Fairgrounds. 1/2-mile dirt. Sprint car event. 10-lap heat: finished 1st. 30-lap feature: finished 1st.

October 8, 1939
Mechanicsburg, PA. Williams Grove Speedway. 1/2-mile clay. Sprint car event. 10-lap heat: finished 2nd. 40-lap feature: finished 7th.

October 15, 1939
Springfield, IL. Illinois State Fairgrounds. 1-mile dirt. Championship car event. Time trial: 38.90 seconds. 3rd fastest time. 100-mile feature: DPO after 30 miles while running 2nd.

1940

Final Standings:
Finished 24th in Eastern AAA Sprint car standings with 139 points; finished 9th in Midwest AAA Sprint car standings with 44 points; finished 16th in AAA National Championship car standings with 135 points; finished 19th in Hankinson Sprint car standings with 305 points; finished 33rd in Hershey, Pennsylvania Stadium standings with 43 points; finished 60th in Eastern AAA Midget car standings with 190 points.

April 28, 1940
Reading, PA. Reading Fairgrounds. 1/2-mile dirt. Sprint car event. 10-lap heat: finished 2nd. 20-lap feature: finished 4th.

May 5, 1940
Mechanicsburg, PA. Williams Grove Speedway. 1/2-mile clay. Sprint car event. 10-lap heat: finished 5th. 15-lap semi: DPO.

May 6, 1940
Hershey, PA. Hershey Stadium. 1/4-mile paved. Midget car event. 10-lap heat: finished 1st. 12-lap semi: finished 3rd. 25-lap feature: DPO.

May 30, 1940
Indianapolis, IN. Indianapolis Motor Speedway. 2 1/2-mile brick and asphalt. Championship car event. Qualified at 122.624 miles per hour. 500-mile feature: DPO after 80 miles. *Struck the outside concrete wall along the front stretch. He received an arm injury. Drove car owned by Joe Marks.*

July 14, 1940
Putnam, CT. Thompson Speedway. 1/2-mile paved. Sprint car event. Time trial: 20.04 seconds. 20-lap feature: DNS.

July 21, 1940
Mechanicsburg, PA. Williams Grove Speedway. 1/2-mile clay. Sprint car event. 10-lap heat: finished 3rd. 40-lap feature: finished 8th.

July 27, 1940
Harrington, DE. Kent-Sussex County Fairgrounds. 1/2-mile dirt. Sprint car event. 30-lap feature: finished 1st.

August 4, 1940
Langhorne, PA. 1-mile dirt. Late model stock car event. 200-mile feature: DNP. *Awarded 19th place.*

August 7, 1940
Union, NJ. 1/2-mile dirt. Sprint car event. 10-lap consolation: finished 1st. 20-lap feature: finished 2nd.

August 8, 1940
Hershey, PA. Hershey Stadium. 1/4-mile paved. Midget car event. 10-lap heat: finished 7th. 15-lap consolation: finished 7th.

August 9, 1940
Freeport, L.I., NY. Freeport Stadium. 1/4-mile paved. 10-lap heat: finished 1st. 12-lap semi: finished 2nd. 40-lap feature: finished 5th.

August 10, 1940
Philadelphia, PA. Baker Bowl. 1/4-mile paved. Midget car event. 10-lap heat: finished 4th.

August 12, 1940
Stapleton, Staten Island, NY. Thompson Stadium. 1/4-mile paved. Midget car event. 10-lap heat: finished 1st.

August 15, 1940
Hershey, PA. Hershey Stadium. 1/4-mile paved. Midget car event. 12-lap consolation: finished 4th. 15-lap semi: finished 6th. 30-lap feature: finished 8th.

August 22, 1940
Milwaukee, WI. Wisconsin State Fairgrounds. 1-mile dirt. Sprint car event. 10-mile heat: finished 4th. 30-mile feature: finished 3rd.

August 24, 1940
Springfield, IL. Illinois State Fairgrounds. 1-mile dirt. Championship car event. Time trial: 38.46 seconds. 2nd fastest time. 100-mile feature: DPO on 44th lap. *Duel in the beginning of race with Rex Mays brought fans to their feet. Mechanic: Frankie DelRoy.*

August 31, 1940
Flemington, NJ. Flemington Fairgrounds. 1/2-mile dirt. Sprint car event. 30-lap feature: finished 2nd.

September 2, 1940
Syracuse, NY. New York State Fairgrounds. 1-mile dirt. Championship car event. 100-mile feature: finished 3rd. *Hinnershitz drove the Gerber Sprint car outfitted with pontoons.*

September 4, 1940
Philadelphia, PA. Baker Bowl. 1/4-mile paved. Midget car event. 12-lap consolation: finished 1st. 25-lap feature: finished 5th.

September 6, 1940
Rutland, VT. 1/2-mile dirt. *Hinnershitz flipped the O'Day Offy during time trial. He received an arm injury. During surgery a steel plate was inserted.*

1941

Final Standings:
Finished 31st in Eastern AAA Sprint car standings with 46 points; finished 4th in CSRA (Central States Racing Association) Sprint car standings with 315 points; finished 3rd in Hankinson Sprint car standings with 858 points.

May 30, 1941
Indianapolis, IN. Indianapolis Motor Speedway. 2 1/2-mile brick and asphalt. Championship car event. Qualified at 121.021 miles per hour. 500-mile feature: finished 10th. Average speed for feature: 105.152 miles per hour. *Relieved by George Robson. Drove car owned by Joe Marks.*

June 22, 1941
Langhorne, PA. 1-mile dirt. Sprint car event. 100-mile feature: finished 7th.

June 29, 1941
Williams Grove, PA. 1/2-mile clay. Sprint car event. 10-lap heat: finished 4th. 12-lap consolation: finished 2nd.

July 4, 1941
Altamont, NY. 1/2-mile dirt. Sprint car event. 10-lap heat: finished 3rd. 30-lap feature: DPO after 14 laps.

July 13, 1941
Williams Grove, PA. 1/2-mile clay. Sprint car event. 10-lap heat: finished 4th. 12-lap consolation: finished 1st. 30-lap feature: finished 5th.

August 2, 1941
Harrington, DE. Kent-Sussex Fairgrounds. 1/2-mile dirt. Sprint car event. Exhibition show. Competed in three match races with Bobby Sall and Ted Horn.

August 16, 1941
Batavia, NY. 1/2-mile dirt. Sprint car event. 10-lap heat: finished 3rd. 20-lap feature: DPO.

August 30, 1941
Flemington, NJ. Flemington Fairgrounds. 1/2-mile dirt. Sprint car event. 10-lap heat: finished 3rd. 20-lap feature: finished 3rd.

September 1, 1941
Flemington, NJ. Flemington Fairgrounds. 1/2-mile dirt. Sprint car event. 10-lap heat: finished 2nd. 25-lap feature: finished 3rd.

September 6, 1941
Dunkirk, NY. 1/2-mile dirt. Sprint car event. 10-lap heat: finished 3rd. 20-lap feature: finished 4th.

September 14, 1941
Dunkirk, NY. 1/2-mile dirt. Sprint car event. 10-lap heat: finished 2nd. 30-lap feature: DPO after 5 laps.

September 20, 1941
Allentown, PA. 1/2-mile dirt. Sprint car event. 10-lap heat: finished 2nd. 30-lap feature: finished 2nd.

September 27, 1941
Bloomsburg, PA. Columbia County Fairgrounds. 1/2-mile dirt. Sprint car event. 10-lap heat: finished 1st. 30-lap feature: finished 2nd.

September 28, 1941
Trenton, NJ. New Jersey State Fairgrounds. 1/2-mile dirt. Sprint car event. 10-lap heat: finished 2nd. 20-lap feature: finished 3rd.

October 1, 1941
Greensboro, NC. 1/2-mile dirt. Sprint car event. 10-lap heat: finished 2nd. 20-lap feature: finished 3rd.

October 4, 1941
Shelby, NC. 1/2-mile dirt. Sprint car event. 10-lap heat: finished 2nd. 20-lap feature: finished 5th.

October 11, 1941
Winston Salem, NC. 1/2-mile dirt. Sprint car event. 10-lap heat: finished 1st. 20-lap feature: finished 2nd.

October 25, 1941
Columbia, SC. 1-mile dirt. Sprint car event. 10-mile feature: finished 4th.

1942

Final Standings:
Finished 2nd in Consolidated Sprint car standings with 208 points.

April 19, 1942
Reading, PA. Reading Fairgrounds. 1/2-mile dirt. Sprint car event. Time trial: 26.56 seconds. 8-lap heat: finished 2nd. 4-lap dash: finished 3rd. 20-lap feature: finished 8th.

May 10, 1942
Langhorne, PA. 1-mile dirt. Sprint car event. Time trial: 36.68 seconds. 8-mile heat: finished 6th. 8-mile heat: finished 3rd. 20-mile feature: finished 4th.

May 17, 1942
Reading, PA. Reading Fairgrounds. 1/2-mile dirt. Sprint car event. Time trial: 27.11 seconds. 10-lap heat: finished 1st. 20-lap feature: finished 3rd.

May 30, 1942
Milwaukee, WI. 1-mile dirt. Sprint car event. 10-mile heat: finished 3rd. 10-mile heat: finished 2nd. 20-mile feature: finished 4th.

June 14, 1942
Davenport, LA. Mississippi Valley Fairgrounds. 1/2-mile dirt. Sprint car event. 10-lap heat: finished 2nd. 20-lap feature: finished 2nd.

July 4, 1942
Birmingham, AL. 1/2-mile dirt. Sprint car event. 8-lap heat: finished 3rd. 20-lap feature: finished 3rd.

1945

September 3, 1945
Hughesville, PA. Lycoming County Fairgrounds. 1/2-mile dirt. Sprint car event. 8-lap heat: finished 2nd. 20-lap feature: finished 2nd.

September 9, 1945
Mechanicsburg, PA. Williams Grove Speedway. 1/2-mile clay. Sprint car event. 10-lap heat: finished 2nd. 40-lap feature: rained out.

September 15, 1945
Altamont, NY. 1/2-mile dirt. Sprint car event. 10-lap heat: finished 2nd. 30-lap feature: DNF. *Hinnershitz hit the guardrail on lap 26 while attempting to take the lead from Bill Holland. He was uninjured.*

September 16, 1945
Hughesville, PA. Lycoming County Fairgrounds. 1/2-mile dirt. Sprint car event. 8-lap heat: finished 2nd. 20-lap feature: finished 3rd.

September 22, 1945
Kutztown, PA. Kutztown Fairgrounds. 1/2-mile dirt. Sprint car event. 10-lap heat: finished 2nd. 25-lap feature: finished 2nd.

September 30, 1945
Mechanicsburg, PA. Williams Grove Speedway. 1/2-mile clay. Sprint car event. 10-lap heat: finished 3rd. 30-lap feature: finished 2nd.

October 6, 1945
Gratz, PA. Gratz Fairgrounds. 1/2-mile dirt. Sprint car event. 10-lap heat: finished 1st. 25-lap feature: finished 4th.

October 13, 1945
Altamont, NY. 1/2-mile dirt. Sprint car event. 10-lap heat: finished 1st. 25-lap feature: finished 2nd.

October 14, 1945
Kutztown, PA. Kutztown Fairgrounds. 1/2-mile dirt. Sprint car event. 10-lap heat: finished 2nd. 25-lap feature: finished 3rd.

October 21, 1945
Mechanicsburg, PA. Williams Grove Speedway. 1/2-mile clay. Sprint car event. 10-lap heat: finished 3rd. 25-lap feature: finished 2nd.

1946

Final Standings:
In 1946 AAA combined both Sprint and Championship points. Hinnershitz finished 5th in AAA National Championship car standings with 896 points.

March 31, 1946
Atlanta, GA. Lakeside Park. 1-mile dirt. Sprint car event. 8-mile consolation: finished 1st. 20-mile feature: DNP.

April 14, 1946
Mechanicsburg, PA. Williams Grove Speedway. 1/2-mile clay. 10-lap heat: finished 3rd. 30-lap feature: finished 9th.

April 28, 1946
Mechanicsburg, PA. Williams Grove Speedway. 1/2-mile clay. Sprint car event. 10-lap heat: finished 4th. 12-lap semi-feature: finished 1st. 30-lap feature: finished 5th.

May 26, 1946
Reading, PA. Reading Fairgrounds. 1/2-mile dirt. Sprint car event. 10-lap heat: finished 2nd. 25-lap feature: finished 4th.

May 30, 1946
Indianapolis, IN. Indianapolis Motor Speedway. 2 1/2-mile brick and asphalt. Championship car event. DNQ. *Mechanical problems. Drove car owned by Milt Marion.*

June 2, 1946
Atlanta, GA. Lakeside Park. 1-mile dirt. Sprint car event. 25-mile feature: finished 5th.

June 9, 1946
Mechanicsburg, PA. Williams Grove Speedway. 1/2-mile clay. Sprint car event. 10-lap heat: finished 2nd. 30-lap feature: finished 5th.

June 16, 1946
Flemington, NJ. Flemington Fairgrounds. 1/2-mile dirt. Sprint car event. 10-lap heat: finished 1st. 25-lap feature: finished 5th.

June 23, 1946
Greensboro, NC. 1/2-mile dirt. Sprint car event. 25-lap feature: finished 4th.

June 30, 1946
Columbus, OH. Powell Speedway. 1/2-mile dirt. Sprint car event. 10-lap heat: finished 1st. 25-lap feature: finished 2nd. *Race flagged at 15 laps due to extreme dust.*

July 7, 1946
Atlanta, GA. Lakewood Park. 1-mile dirt. Sprint car event. 50-mile feature: finished 2nd.

July 14, 1946
Reading, PA. Reading Fairgrounds. 1/2-mile dirt. Sprint car event. 10-lap heat: finished 4th. 10-lap consolation: finished 2nd. 25-lap feature: finished 3rd.

July 20, 1946
DuBois, PA. 1/2-mile dirt. Sprint car event. 20-lap feature: finished 2nd.

July 21, 1946
Langhorne, PA. 1-mile dirt. Sprint car event. 10-mile heat: finished 4th. 10-mile consolation: finished 1st. 20-mile feature: finished 5th.

July 28, 1946
Mechanicsburg, PA. Williams Grove Speedway. 1/2-mile clay. Sprint car event. 10-lap heat: finished 2nd. 30-lap feature: finished 4th.

August 4, 1946
Columbus, OH. Powell Speedway. 1/2-mile dirt. Sprint car event. 10-lap heat: finished 1st. 30-lap feature: finished 4th.

August 10, 1946
Bedford, PA. Bedford Fairgrounds. 1/2-mile dirt. Sprint car event. 10-lap heat: finished 2nd. 20-lap feature: finished 3rd.

August 11, 1946
Batavia, NY. 1/2-mile dirt. Sprint car event. 20-lap feature: finished 3rd.

August 24, 1946
Hamburg, NY. Erie County Fairgrounds. 1/2-mile dirt. Sprint car event. 10-lap heat: finished 2nd. 20-lap feature: finished 5th.

August 25, 1946
Uniontown, PA. 1/2-mile dirt. Sprint car event. 10-lap heat: finished 2nd. 20-lap feature: finished 2nd.

August 31, 1946
Hamburg, NY. Erie County Fairgrounds. 1/2-mile dirt. Sprint car event. 10-lap heat: finished 2nd. 20-lap feature: finished 2nd.

September 1, 1946
Flemington, NJ. Flemington Fairgrounds. 1/2-mile dirt. Sprint car event. 20-lap feature: finished 2nd.

September 6, 1946
Rutland, VT. 1/2-mile dirt. Sprint car event. 8-lap heat: finished 2nd. 20-lap feature: finished 4th.

September 7, 1946
Port Royal, PA. 1/2-mile dirt. Sprint car event. 8-lap heat: finished 2nd. 16-lap feature: finished 2nd.

September 8, 1946
Mechanicsburg, PA. Williams Grove Speedway. 1/2-mile clay. Sprint car event. 10-lap heat: finished 2nd. 30-lap feature: finished 3rd.

September 15, 1946
Reading, PA. Reading Fairgrounds. 1/2-mile dirt. Sprint car event. Time trial: 26.62 seconds. 10-lap heat: finished 1st. Time of heat: 4:34.71 minutes. New track record. 25-lap feature: finished 2nd.

September 21, 1946
Allentown, PA. Allentown Fairgrounds. 1/2-mile dirt. Sprint car event. 8-lap heat: finished 1st. 20-lap feature: finished 2nd.

September 29, 1946
Trenton, NJ. New Jersey State Fairgrounds. 1-mile dirt. Sprint car event. 8-mile heat: finished 2nd. 20-mile feature: finished 4th.

October 19, 1946
Raleigh, NC. 1/2-mile dirt. Sprint car event. 20-lap feature: finished 3rd.

October 27, 1946
Mechanicsburg, PA. Williams Grove Speedway. 1/2-mile clay. Sprint car event. 10-lap heat: finished 2nd. 50-lap feature: finished 5th.

November 3, 1946
Richmond, VA. Richmond Fairgrounds. 1/2-mile dirt. Sprint car event. 10-lap heat: finished 1st. 25-lap feature: finished 1st.

1947

Final Standings:
Finished 3rd in Eastern AAA Sprint car standings with 691 points; finished 3rd in Midwest AAA Sprint car standings with 190 points.

April 13, 1947
Trenton, NJ. New Jersey State Fairgrounds. 1-mile dirt. Sprint car event. Time trial: 42.87 seconds. 8-mile heat: finished 1st. 20-mile feature: finished 2nd.

April 19, 1947
Richmond, VA. Richmond Fairgrounds. 1/2-mile dirt. Sprint car event. 10-lap heat: finished 1st. 20-lap feature: DNP.

April 20, 1947
Mechanicsburg, PA. Williams Grove Speedway. 1/2-mile clay. Sprint car event. Time trial: 27.10 seconds. 10-lap heat: finished 2nd. 30-lap feature: finished 6th.

April 26, 1947
Richmond, VA. Richmond Fairgrounds. 1/2-mile dirt. Sprint car event. Time trial: 26.00 seconds. 8-lap heat: finished 1st. 20-lap feature: finished 6th.

April 27, 1947
Reading, PA. Reading Fairgrounds. 1/2-mile dirt. Sprint car event. Time trial: 27.70 seconds. 10-lap heat: finished 2nd. 25-lap feature: finished 5th.

May 4, 1947
Mechanicsburg, PA. Williams Grove Speedway. 1/2-mile clay. Sprint car event. 12-lap consolation: finished 1st. 30-lap feature: finished 3rd.

May 11, 1947
Langhorne, PA. 1-mile dirt. Sprint car event. Time trial 37:15 seconds. 10-mile heat: finished 2nd. 20-mile feature: finished 2nd.

May 30, 1947
Bedford, PA. Bedford Fairgrounds. 1/2-mile dirt. Sprint car event. 10-lap heat: finished 2nd. 20-lap feature: finished 1st.

June 1, 1947
Reading, PA. Reading Fairgrounds. 1/2-mile dirt. Sprint car event. 10 lap heat: finished 1st. 25-lap feature: DPO on the 1st lap.

June 15, 1947
Mechanicsburg, PA. Williams Grove, PA. 1/2-mile clay. Sprint car event. Time trial: 28.23 seconds. 10-lap heat: finished 2nd. 30-lap feature: DPO.

June 22, 1947
Salem, IN. 1/2-mile high-banked dirt. Sprint car event. 20-lap feature: finished 1st. *This was the first race ever run at Salem Speedway.*

June 29, 1947
Columbus, OH. Powell Speedway. 1/2-mile dirt. Sprint car event. 10-lap heat: finished 2nd. 20-lap feature: finished 1st.

July 4, 1947
Salem, IN. 1/2-mile high-banked dirt. Sprint car event. 20-lap feature: finished 1st.

July 6, 1947
Mechanicsburg, PA. Williams Grove Speedway. 1/2-mile clay. Sprint car event. Time trial: 27.76 seconds. 10-lap heat: finished 2nd. 30-lap feature: DPO on 21st lap while running 3rd. *Hinnershitz tangled with Earl Johns on the 1st lap before restarting.*

July 27, 1947
Mechanicsburg, PA. Williams Grove Speedway. 1/2-mile clay. Sprint car event. Time trial: 27.33 seconds. 10-lap heat: finished 1st. 30-lap feature: finished 2nd.

August 3, 1947
Salem, IN. 1/2-mile high-banked dirt. Sprint car event. 30-lap feature: finished 1st.

August 10, 1947
Winchester, IN. 1/2-mile high-banked dirt. Sprint car event. 20-lap feature: finished 2nd.

August 17, 1947
Mechanicsburg, PA. Williams Grove Speedway. 1/2-mile clay. Sprint car event. Time trial: 27.36 seconds. 10-lap heat: finished 2nd. 30-lap feature: finished 1st.

August 21, 1947
Milwaukee, WI. 1-mile dirt. Sprint car event. Time trial: 39.28 seconds. 10-mile heat: finished 1st. 20-mile feature: finished 2nd.

August 22, 1947
Milwaukee, WI. 1-mile dirt. Sprint car event. 10-mile heat: finished 2nd. 20-mile feature: DPO on 3rd lap.

August 24, 1947
Hatfield, PA. Montgomery County Fairgrounds. 1/2-mile dirt. Sprint car event. Time trial: 25.70 seconds. 8-lap heat: finished 1st. 16-lap feature: finished 1st.

August 27, 1947
Mechanicsburg, PA. Williams Grove, PA. 1/2-mile clay. Sprint car event. 10-lap heat: finished 2nd. 30-lap feature: finished 5th.

August 31, 1947
Putnam, CT. Thompson Speedway. 1/2-mile paved. Sprint car event. 10-lap heat: finished 3rd. 25-lap feature: finished 4th.

September 5, 1947
Rutland, VT. 1/2-mile dirt. Sprint car event. 8-lap heat: finished 3rd. 20-lap feature: finished 2nd.

September 6, 1947
Port Royal, PA. 1/2-mile dirt. Sprint car event. 10-lap heat: finished 1st. 20-lap feature: finished 2nd.

September 7, 1947
Dayton, OH. 1/2-mile high-banked paved. Sprint car event. 10-lap heat: finished 1st. 20-lap feature: finished 2nd.

September 10, 1947
Mechanicsburg, PA. Williams Grove Speedway. 1/2-mile clay. Sprint car event. 10-lap heat: finished 1st. 30-lap feature: finished 2nd.

September 12, 1947
Uniontown, PA. 1/2-mile dirt. Sprint car event. 10-lap heat: finished 2nd. 25-lap feature: finished 1st.

September 13, 1947
Washington, PA. Arden Downs. 1/2-mile dirt. Sprint car event. 10-lap heat: finished 1st. 20-lap feature: finished 2nd.

September 14, 1947
Reading, PA. Reading Fairgrounds. 1/2-mile dirt. Sprint car event. 10-lap heat: finished 1st. 25-lap feature: DPO.

September 19, 1947
Springfield, MA. 1/2-mile paved. Sprint car event. 10-lap heat: finished 2nd. 20-lap feature: finished 5th.

September 20, 1947
Allentown, PA. Allentown Fairgrounds. 1/2-mile dirt. Sprint car event. Time trial: 27.29 seconds. 10-lap heat: finished 1st. 20-lap feature: finished 1st.

September 21, 1947
Dover, NJ. 1/2-mile banked dirt. Sprint car event. 30-lap feature: finished 2nd.

September 26, 1947
Uniontown, PA. 1/2-mile banked dirt. Sprint car event. Time trial: 21:33 seconds. 10-lap heat: finished 1st. 25-lap feature: DPO.

October 19, 1947
Mechanicsburg, PA. Williams Grove Speedway. 1/2-mile clay. Sprint car event. Time trial: 27.04 seconds. 10-lap heat: finished 2nd. 50-lap feature: finished 2nd.

November 9, 1947
Atlanta, GA. Lakewood Park. 1-mile dirt. Sprint car event. 8-mile heat: finished 1st. 20-mile feature: DPO after 8 miles.

November 16, 1947
Jacksonville, FL. 1/2-mile dirt. Sprint car event. Time trial: 24.96 seconds. 10-lap heat: finished 2nd. 20-lap feature: finished 3rd.

November 30, 1947
Macon, GA. Central Park. 1/2-mile dirt. Sprint car event. 20-lap feature: finished 6th. *Hinnershitz intentionally slowed down after running 2nd for 16 laps.*

1948

Final Standings:
Finished 2nd in Eastern AAA Sprint car standings with 706 points; finished 6th in Midwest AAA Sprint car standings with 123 points; finished 24th in AAA National Championship car standings with 200 points.

March 21, 1948
Atlanta, GA. Lakewood Park. 1-mile dirt. Sprint car event. 10-mile heat: finished 2nd. 20-mile feature: finished 4th.

April 4, 1948
Reading, PA. Reading Fairgrounds. 1/2-mile dirt. Sprint car event. Time trial: 24.35 seconds. New track record. 10-lap heat: finished 1st. 25-lap feature: DNS.

April 17, 1948
Mechanicsburg, PA. Williams Grove Speedway. 1/2-mile clay. Sprint car event. 10-lap heat: finished 3rd. 30-lap feature: finished 2nd.

April 18, 1948
Trenton, NJ. New Jersey State Fairgrounds. 1-mile dirt. Sprint car event. 8-mile heat: finished 1st. 25-mile feature: DNS.

May 2, 1948
Reading, PA. Reading Fairgrounds. 1/2-mile dirt. Sprint car event. 10-lap heat: finished 1st. 25 lap feature: finished 2nd.

May 9, 1948
Trenton, NJ. New Jersey State Fairgrounds. 1-mile dirt. Sprint car event. 20-mile feature: finished 2nd.

May 23, 1948
Richmond, VA. 1/2-mile dirt. Sprint car event. 10-lap heat: finished 1st. 25-lap feature: finished 2nd.

May 30, 1948
Indianapolis, IN. Indianapolis Motor Speedway. 2 1/2-mile brick and asphalt. Championship car event. Qualified at 125.122 miles per hour. 500-mile feature: finished 9th. *Hinnershitz was flagged at 199 laps. Drove car owned by Ed Walsh.*

June 6, 1948
Mechanicsburg, PA. Williams Grove Speedway. 1/2-mile clay. Sprint car event. 10-lap heat: finished 1st. 30-lap feature: finished 1st.

June 12, 1948
Mineola, L.I., NY. Nassau County Fairgrounds. 1/2-mile dirt. Sprint car event. 10-lap consolation: finished 1st. 25-lap feature: finished 3rd.

July 11, 1948
Mechanicsburg, PA. Williams Grove Speedway. 1/2-mile clay. Sprint car event. 10-lap heat: finished 1st. 30-lap feature: DPO after 27 laps.

July 25, 1948
Selinsgrove, PA. Snyder County Fairgrounds. 1/2-mile banked dirt. Sprint car event. 20-lap feature: finished 1st.

August 8, 1948
Martinsville, VA. 1/2-mile dirt. Sprint car event. 10-lap heat: finished 1st. 25-lap feature: finished 2nd.

August 10, 1948
Milwaukee, WI. 1-mile dirt. Sprint car event. 10-mile heat: finished 3rd. 25-mile feature: finished 4th.

August 11, 1948
Milwaukee, WI. 1-mile dirt. Sprint car event. 30-mile feature: finished 2nd.

August 14, 1948
Bedford, PA. Bedford Fairgrounds. 1/2-mile dirt. Sprint car event.
10-lap heat: finished 1st. 20-lap feature: DPO after 10 laps.

August 29, 1948
Salem, IN. 1/2-mile high-banked dirt. Sprint car event. 10-lap heat:
finished 1st. 20-lap feature: finished 1st. *Race was flagged at 11 laps
due to accident.*

September 5, 1948
Flemington, NJ. Flemington Fairgrounds. 1/2-mile dirt. Sprint car
event. 25-lap feature: finished 1st.

September 12, 1948
Mechanicsburg, PA. Williams Grove Speedway. 1/2-mile clay. Sprint
car event. 10-lap heat: finished 2nd. 30-lap feature: finished 1st.

September 13, 1948
Rutland, VT. 1/2-mile dirt. Sprint car event. 10-lap heat: finished
2nd. 20-lap feature: finished 1st.

September 19, 1948
Reading, PA. Reading Fairgrounds. 1/2-mile dirt. Sprint car event.
10-lap heat: finished 2nd. 20-lap feature: finished 2nd.

September 24, 1948
Springfield, MA. 1/2-mile dirt. Sprint car event. 10-lap heat: finished 2nd. 15-lap feature: finished 2nd.

September 25, 1948
Allentown, PA. Allentown Fairgrounds. 1/2-mile dirt. Sprint car
event. 10-lap heat: finished 1st. 20-lap feature: finished 1st.

September 26, 1948
Dayton, OH. 1/2-mile high-banked paved. Sprint car event. 10-lap
heat: finished 2nd. 20-lap feature: finished 1st.

October 3, 1948
Trenton, NJ. New Jersey State Fairgrounds. 1-mile dirt. Sprint Car event. Time trial: 40.40 seconds. 8-mile heat: finished 1st. 20-mile feature: DNS.

October 9, 1948
Charlotte, NC. Charlotte Fairgrounds. 1/2-mile dirt. Sprint car event. 10-lap heat: finished 1st. 20-lap feature: finished 1st.

October 10, 1948
Mechanicsburg, PA. Williams Grove Speedway. 1/2-mile clay. Sprint car event. 10-lap heat: finished 1st. 30-feature: DPO after 15 laps.

October 24, 1948
Mechanicsburg, PA. Williams Grove Speedway. 1/2-mile clay. Sprint car event. 10-lap heat: DPO. 50-lap feature: finished 5th. *Hinnershitz replaced Mark Light in the feature.*

1949

Final Standings:
Finished 1st in Eastern AAA Sprint car standings with 701 points; finished 9th in Midwest AAA Sprint car standings with 98 points; finished 37th in AAA National Championship car standings with 117 points.

April 3, 1949
Reading, PA. Reading Fairgrounds. 1/2-mile dirt. Sprint car event. 10-lap heat: finished 1st. 25-lap feature: finished 1st.

April 21, 1949
Indianapolis, IN. Indianapolis Motor Speedway. Championship car event. 2 1/2-mile brick and asphalt. *Hinnershitz crashed during practice, hitting the wall and suffering head injuries. He drove a car owned by Milt Marion. Sam Hanks drove the car in the race and DPO after 20 laps.*

April 24, 1949
Mechanicsburg, PA. Williams Grove Speedway. 1/2-mile clay. Sprint car event. 10-lap heat: finished 1st. 30-lap feature: finished 1st.

May 29, 1949
Winchester, IN. 1/2-mile high-banked paved. Sprint car event. Time trial: 22.79 seconds. 10-lap consolation: finished 1st. 20-lap feature: finished 5th.

June 12, 1949
Heidelberg, PA. 1/2-mile dirt. Sprint car event. Time trial: 23.44 seconds. 10-lap heat: finished 1st. 30-lap feature: finished 1st.

July 10, 1949
Dayton, OH. 1/2-mile high-banked paved. Sprint car event. Time trial: 22:13 seconds. 10-lap heat: finished 1st. 20-lap feature: finished 6th.

July 24, 1949
Salem, IN. 1/2-mile high-banked paved. Sprint car event. Time trial: 22:94 seconds. 10-lap heat: finished 2nd. 20-lap feature: finished 4th.

July 31, 1949
Mechanicsburg, PA. Williams Grove Speedway. 1/2-mile clay. Championship car event. 10-lap heat: finished 3rd. 50-lap feature: DPO after 11 laps.

August 13, 1949
Bedford, PA. Bedford Fairgrounds. 1/2-mile dirt. Sprint car event. 10-lap heat: finished 2nd. 20-lap feature: finished 1st. Time of feature: 9:08.81 minutes. New track record.

August 20, 1949
Middletown, NY. Orange County Fairgrounds. 1/2-mile dirt. Sprint car event. Time trial. 26.05 seconds. New track record. 10-lap heat: finished 1st. 20-lap feature: finished 1st. Time of feature: 9:56.01 minutes. New track record.

August 21, 1949
Mechanicsburg, PA. Williams Grove Speedway. Sprint car event. 10-lap heat: finished 1st. 30-lap feature: finished 1st.

August 26, 1949
Milwaukee, WI. 1-mile dirt. Sprint car event. 10-mile heat: finished 4th. 25-mile feature: DPO.

August 27, 1949
St. Paul, MN. 1/2-mile dirt. Sprint car event. 10-lap heat: finished 3rd. 30-lap feature: finished 1st.

August 28, 1949
St. Paul, MN. 1/2-mile dirt. Sprint car event. DNS. *Mechanical problems.*

September 10, 1949
Syracuse, NY. New York State Fairgounds. 1-mile dirt. Championship car event. 100-mile feature: finished 10th. *Hinnershitz relieved Emil Andres in the feature.*

September 18, 1949
Reading, PA. Reading Fairgrounds. 1/2-mile dirt. Sprint car event. 10-lap heat: finished 1st. 20-lap feature: finished 1st.

September 24, 1949
Allentown, PA. 1/2-mile dirt. Sprint car event. 10-lap heat: finished 1st. 20-lap feature: finished 3rd.

September 25, 1949
Mechanicsburg, PA. Williams Grove Speedway. 1/2-mile clay. Sprint car event. 10-lap heat: finished 1st. 30-lap feature: finished 4th.

October 2, 1949
Trenton, NJ. New Jersey State Fairgrounds. 1-mile dirt. Sprint car event. 8-mile heat: finished 2nd. 20-mile feature: finished 2nd.

October 16, 1949
Langhorne, PA. 1-mile dirt. Championship car event. Time trial: 36:18 seconds. 100-mile feature: finished 5th.

October 22, 1949
Richmond, VA. 1/2-mile dirt. Sprint car event. 20-lap feature: finished 1st. Time of feature: 9:09.00 minutes. New track record.

October 23, 1949
Mechanicsburg, PA. Williams Grove Speedway. 1/2-mile clay. Sprint car event. 10-lap heat: finished 3rd. 50-lap feature: finished 4th.

October 30, 1949
Owego, NY. Shangra-La Speedway. 1/2-mile oiled dirt. Sprint car event. 10-lap heat: finished 1st. 25-lap feature: finished 1st.

1950

Final Standings:
Finished 1st in Eastern AAA Sprint car standings with 746 points; finished 13th in Midwest AAA Sprint car standings with 67 points.

April 2, 1950
Reading, PA. Reading Fairgrounds. 1/2-mile dirt. Sprint car event. 10-lap heat: finished 1st. 30-lap feature: finished 1st. Time of feature: 13:39.41 minutes. New track record.

April 16, 1950
Mechanicsburg, PA. Williams Grove Speedway. 1/2-mile clay. Sprint car event. 10-lap heat: finished 3rd. 30-lap feature: finished 2nd.

May 7, 1950
Atlanta, GA. Lakewood Park. 1-mile dirt. Sprint car event. 8-mile heat: finished 1st. 25-mile feature: finished 1st.

May 14, 1950
Greensboro, NC. 1/2-mile dirt. Sprint car event. 10-lap heat: finished 1st. 30-lap feature: finished 1st.

May 21, 1950
Mechanicsburg, PA. Williams Grove Speedway. 1/2-mile clay. Sprint car event. 10-lap heat: finished 2nd. 30-lap feature: finished 1st.

June 4, 1950
Trenton, NJ. New Jersey State Fairgrounds. 1-mile dirt. Sprint car event. 8-mile heat: finished 1st. 25-mile feature: finished 1st.

June 11, 1950
Mechanicsburg, PA. Williams Grove Speedway. 1/2-mile clay. Sprint car event. 10-lap heat: finished 2nd. 30-lap feature: DPO after 20 laps.

June 18, 1950
Reading, PA. Reading Fairgrounds. 1/2-mile dirt. Sprint car event. 10-lap heat: finished 1st. 30-lap feature: finished 2nd.

July 2, 1950
Mechanicsburg, PA. Williams Grove Speedway. 1/2-mile clay. Sprint car event. 10-lap heat: finished 1st. 30-lap feature: finished 1st.

July 4, 1950
Atlanta, GA. Lakewood Park. 1-mile dirt. Sprint car event. *Hinnershitz crashed on the 3rd lap of heat race. A blowout of the car's right rear tire caused him to go out over the embankment and flip in the second turn. He was hospitalized for treatment of a slight fracture of the pelvis.*

July 29, 1950
Harrington, DE. Kent-Sussex Fairgrounds. 1/2-mile dirt. Sprint car event. 10-lap heat: finished 2nd. 20-lap feature: finished 2nd.

July 30, 1950
Mechanicsburg, PA. Williams Grove Speedway. 1/2-mile clay. Sprint car event. 10-lap heat: finished 2nd. 30-lap feature: finished 1st.

August 12, 1950
Cedar Rapids, IA. 1/2-mile dirt. Sprint car event. 10-lap heat: finished 1st. 25-lap feature: finished 4th.

August 14, 1950
Mechanicsburg, PA. Williams Grove Speedway. 1/2-mile clay. Championship car event. 10-lap consolation: finished 5th. 50-lap feature: finished 8th.

August 20, 1950
Hamburg, NY. Erie County Fairgrounds. 1/2-mile dirt. Sprint car event. 20-lap feature: finished 3rd.

August 26, 1950
St. Paul, MN. 1/2-mile dirt. Sprint car event. 10-lap heat: finished 1st. 25-lap feature: finished 4th.

August 27, 1950
St. Paul, MN. 1/2-mile dirt. Sprint car event. 10-lap heat: finished 2nd. 25-lap feature: finished 1st.

September 3, 1950
Essex Junction, VT. 1/2-mile dirt. Sprint car event. 10-lap heat: finished 2nd. 20-lap feature: finished 2nd.

September 4, 1950
Altamont, NY. 1/2-mile dirt. Sprint car event. Time trial: 25.05 seconds. New track record. 10-lap heat: finished 1st. Time of heat: 3:27.89 minutes. New track record. 25-lap feature: finished 1st. Time of feature: 11:11.95 minutes. New track record.

September 8, 1950
Rutland, VT. 1/2-mile dirt. Sprint car event. 10-lap heat: finished 2nd. 20-lap feature: finished 2nd.

September 9, 1950
Port Royal, PA. 1/2-mile dirt. Sprint car event. 10-lap heat: finished 1st. 20-lap feature: finished 1st.

September 17, 1950
Reading, PA. Reading Fairgrounds. 1/2-mile dirt. Sprint car event. 10-lap heat: finished 1st. 20-lap feature: DPO after 7 laps.

September 22, 1950
Springfield, MA. 1/2-mile dirt. Sprint car event. 10-lap heat: finished 1st. 16-lap feature: finished 2nd.

September 23, 1950
Springfield, MA. 1/2-mile dirt. Sprint car event. 10-lap heat: finished 1st. 20-lap feature: finished 2nd.

October 3, 1950
Trenton, NJ. New Jersey State Fairgrounds. 1-mile dirt. Sprint car event. 8-mile heat: finished 1st. 25-mile feature: finished 1st.

October 8, 1950
Charlotte, NC. 1/2-mile dirt. Sprint car event. 10 lap heat: finished 1st. 20-lap feature: finished 1st.

October 21, 1950
Raleigh, NC. 1/2-mile dirt. Sprint car event. 10-lap heat: finished 1st. 20-lap feature: finished 4th.

October 22, 1950
Mechanicsburg, PA. Williams Grove Speedway. 1/2-mile clay. Sprint car event. 10-lap heat: finished 3rd. 50-lap feature: finished 2nd.

1951

Final Standings:
Finished 1st in Eastern AAA Sprint car standings with 678 points; finished 26th in Midwest AAA Sprint car standings with 28 points.

April 8, 1951
Reading, PA. Reading Fairgrounds. 1/2-mile dirt. Sprint car event. 10-lap heat: finished 2nd. 30-lap feature: finished 3rd.

April 15, 1951
Mechanicsburg, PA. Williams Grove Speedway. 1/2-mile clay. Sprint car event. 10-lap heat: finished 3rd. 30-lap feature: finished 4th.

April 22, 1951
Trenton, NJ. New Jersey State Fairgrounds. 1-mile dirt. Sprint car event. 8-mile heat: finished 2nd. 25-mile feature: finished 3rd.

April 29, 1951
Mechanicsburg, PA. Williams Grove Speedway. 1/2-mile clay. Sprint car event. 10-lap heat: finished 1st. 30-lap feature: finished 3rd.

May 6 1951
Savannah, GA. Oglethorpe Speedway. 1/2-mile dirt. Sprint car event. 20-lap feature: finished 3rd.

May 13, 1951
Mechanicsburg, PA. Williams Grove Speedway. 1/2-mile clay. Sprint car event. 10-lap heat: finished 1st. 30-lap feature: finished 3rd.

June 3, 1951
Reading, PA. Reading Fairgrounds. 1/2-mile dirt. Sprint car event. 10-lap heat: finished 1st. 30-lap feature: finished 3rd.

June 10, 1951
Toledo, OH. Raceway Park. 1/2-mile banked dirt. Sprint car event. 10-lap heat: finished 2nd. 30-lap feature: finished 2nd.

June 17, 1951
Mechanicsburg, PA. Williams Grove Speedway. 1/2-mile clay. Sprint car event. 10-lap heat: finished 3rd. 30-lap feature: DPO after 7 laps.

June 24, 1951
Langhorne, PA. 1-mile dirt. Championship car event. Time trial: 38.96 seconds. 100-mile feature: DNQ.

July 30, 1951
Mechanicsburg, PA. Williams Grove Speedway. 1/2-mile clay. Championship car event. 10-lap heat: finished 2nd. 50-lap feature: finished 4th.

August 11, 1951
Bedford, PA. Bedford Fairgrounds. 1/2-mile dirt. Sprint car event. 10-lap heat: finished 1st. 20-lap feature: finished 6th.

August 26, 1951
St. Paul, MN. 1/2-mile dirt. Sprint car event. 25-lap feature: finished 2nd.

August 27, 1951
St. Paul, MN. 1/2-mile dirt. Sprint car event. 10-lap heat: finished 1st. 25-lap feature: finished 2nd.

September 1, 1951
Essex Junction, VT. 1/2-mile dirt. Sprint car event. Time trial: 26.05 seconds. 10-lap heat: finished 1st. 20-lap feature: finished 2nd.

September 4, 1951
Flemington, NJ. Flemington Fairgrounds. 1/2-mile dirt. Sprint car event. 10-lap heat: finished 3rd. 20-lap feature: finished 3rd.

September 8, 1951
Syracuse, NY. New York State Fairgrounds. 1-mile dirt. Championship car event. Time trial: 39.17 seconds. 100-mile feature: DNP. *Mechanical problems; awarded 14th place.*

September 9, 1951
Mechanicsburg, PA. Williams Grove Speedway. 1/2-mile clay. Sprint car event. 10-lap heat: finished 1st. 30-lap feature: finished 1st. Time of feature: 13:21.27 minutes. New track record.

September 16, 1951
Reading, PA. Reading Fairgrounds. 1/2-mile dirt. Sprint car event. 10-lap heat: finished 1st. 20-lap feature: finished 3rd.

September 21, 1951
Springfield, MA. 1/2-mile dirt. Sprint car event. 10-lap consolation: finished 1st. 20-lap feature: finished 2nd.

September 22, 1951
Springfield, MA. 1/2-mile dirt. Sprint car event. Time trial: 25.14 seconds. New track record. 10-lap heat: finished 2nd. 20-lap feature: finished 1st. *Race flagged at 12 laps due to rain.*

September 23, 1951
Mechanicsburg, PA. Williams Grove Speedway. 1/2-mile clay. Sprint car event. 10-lap heat: finished 2nd. 30-lap feature: finished 1st.

September 30, 1951
Trenton, NJ. New Jersey State Fairgrounds. 1-mile dirt. Sprint car event. 8-mile heat: finished 1st. 25-mile feature: finished 1st. Time of feature: 18:37.21 minutes. New track record.

October 6, 1951
Charlotte, NC. 1/2-mile dirt. Sprint car event. 20-lap feature: finished 3rd.

October 13, 1951
Atlanta, GA. Lakewood Park. 1-mile dirt. Sprint car event. 10-mile heat: finished 1st. 25-mile feature: finished 1st. Time of feature: 16:51.02 minutes. New track record.

October 20, 1951
Raleigh, NC. 1/2-mile dirt. Sprint car event. 10-lap heat: finished 1st. 20-lap feature: finished 1st. Time of feature: 9:04.80 minutes. New track record.

October 21, 1951
Mechanicsburg, PA. Williams Grove Speedway. 1/2-mile clay. Sprint car event. 10-lap heat: finished 1st. 50-lap feature: finished 3rd.

November 25, 1951
Tampa, FL. 1/2-mile dirt. Time trial: 23.11 seconds. New track record. 10-lap heat: finished 1st. Time of heat: 4:03.51 minutes. New track record. 30-lap feature: finished 1st. Time of feature: 12:28.33 minutes. New track record.

December 2, 1951
West Palm Beach, FL. 1/2-mile dirt. Sprint car event. 10-lap heat: finished 2nd. 20-lap feature: finished 4th.

December 9, 1951
Tampa, FL. Sprint car event. Time trial: 22.90 seconds. New track record. DNS. *Broken drive shaft.*

1952

Final Standings:
Finished 1st in Eastern AAA Sprint car standings with 601 points; finished 14th in Midwest AAA Sprint car standings with 196 points; finished 40th in AAA National Championship car standings with 40 points.

April 6, 1952
Reading, PA. Reading Fairgrounds. 1/2-mile dirt. Sprint car event. 10-lap heat: finished 3rd. 30-lap feature: finished 1st. *Race was flagged at 23 laps.*

April 20, 1952
Mechanicsburg, PA. Williams Grove Speedway. 1/2-mile clay. Sprint car event. 10-lap heat: finished 1st. 30-lap feature: finished 1st. Time of feature: 13:18.91 minutes. New track record.

May 4, 1952
Mechanicsburg, PA. Williams Grove Speedway. 1/2-mile clay. Sprint car event. 10-lap heat: finished 1st. 30-lap feature: finished 2nd.

June 1, 1952
Mechanicsburg, PA. Williams Grove Speedway. 1/2-mile clay. Sprint car event. 10-lap heat: finished 1st. 20-lap feature: finished 1st.

June 8, 1952
Moundsville, WV. 1/2-mile dirt. Sprint car event. Time trial: 25.63 seconds. New track record. 10-lap heat: finished 1st. 20-lap feature: finished 2nd.

June 15, 1952
Mechanicsburg, PA. Williams Grove Speedway. 1/2-mile clay. Sprint car event. 10-lap heat: finished 1st. 30-lap feature: finished 5th.

July 4, 1952
Dunkirk, NY. 1/2-mile dirt. Sprint car event. Time trial: 26.48 seconds. New track record. 10-lap heat: finished 2nd. 20-lap feature: finished 1st. Time of feature: 9:23.76 minutes. New track record.

July 6, 1952
Mechanicsburg, PA. Williams Grove Speedway. 1/2-mile clay. Late model stock car event. 200-lap feature - AAA Stock Car Classic: DPO after 172 laps.

July 13, 1952
Mechanicsburg, PA. Williams Grove Speedway. 1/2-mile clay. Sprint car event. 10-lap heat: finished 2nd. 30-lap feature: finished 6th.

July 20, 1952
Terre Haute, IN. 1/2-mile dirt. Sprint car event. 10-lap heat: finished 2nd. 30-lap feature: finished 1st.

July 26, 1952
Harrington, DE. Kent-Sussex County Fairgrounds. 1/2-mile dirt. Sprint car event. Time trial: 23.75 seconds. New track record. 10-lap heat: finished 1st. Time of heat: 3:33.57 minutes. New track record. 20-lap feature: finished 1st.

July 27, 1952
Mechanicsburg, PA. Williams Grove Speedway. 1/2-mile clay. Championship car event. 50-lap feature: DPO after 12 laps.

August 3, 1952
Richmond, VA. 1/2-mile dirt. Late model stock car event. 200-lap feature - AAA Stock Car Classic: DNP. *Drove a Nash Rambler.*

August 9, 1952
Bedford, PA. 1/2-mile dirt. Sprint car event. 10-lap heat: finished 3rd. 20-lap feature: DPO after 7 laps.

August 10, 1952
Hughesville, PA. Lycoming County Fairgrounds. 1/2-mile dirt. Sprint car event. 10-lap heat: finished 2nd. 20-lap feature: finished 2nd.

August 16, 1952
Springfield, IL. 1-mile dirt. Championship car event. 100-mile feature: finished 9th.

August 19, 1952
Cedar Rapids, IA. 1/2-mile dirt. Sprint car event. DNS. *Mechanical trouble.*

August 25, 1952
St. Paul, MN. 1/2-mile dirt. Sprint car event. 10-lap heat: finished 2nd. 25-lap feature: finished 2nd.

August 26, 1952
St. Paul, MN. 1/2-mile dirt. Sprint car event. 10-lap heat: finished 1st. 20-lap feature: DPO after 8 laps.

August 31, 1952
Essex Junction, VT. 1/2-mile dirt. Sprint car event. 10-lap heat: finished 1st. 16-lap feature: finished 1st.

September 2, 1952
Richmond, VA. 1/2-mile dirt. Sprint car event. 10-lap heat: finished 2nd. 30-lap feature: finished 1st. Time of feature: 12:49.60 minutes. New track record.

September 6, 1952
Rutland, VT. 1/2-mile dirt. Sprint car event. 20-lap feature: DNF. *Spun out on 4th lap.*

September 7, 1952
Mechanicsburg, PA. Williams Grove Speedway. 1/2-mile clay. Sprint car event. 10-lap heat finished 1st. 30-lap feature: finished 3rd.

September 13, 1952
Morristown, NJ. 1/2-mile paved. Sprint car event. 10-lap heat: finished 3rd. 25-lap feature: finished 3rd.

September 14, 1952
Reading, PA. Reading Fairgrounds. 1/2-mile dirt. Sprint car event. 10-lap heat; finished 1st. 20-lap feature: finished 2nd.

September 20, 1952
Allentown, PA. Allentown Fairgrounds. 1/2-mile dirt. Sprint car event. Time trial: 24.65 seconds. New track record. 10-lap heat: finished 1st. 20-lap feature: finished 1st. Time of feature: 9:04.23 minutes. New track record.

September 21, 1952
Terre Haute, IN. Vigo County Fairgrounds. 1/2-mile dirt. Sprint car event. 10-lap heat: finished 1st. 30-lap feature: finished 3rd.

September 27, 1952
Richmond, VA. 1/2-mile dirt. Sprint car event. 10-lap heat: finished 1st. 20-lap feature: finished 1st.

September 28, 1952
Trenton, NJ. New Jersey State Fairgrounds. 1-mile dirt. Sprint car event. Time trial: 39.83 seconds. New track record. 8-mile heat: finished 1st. 25-mile feature: finished 1st. Time of feature: 18:30.59 minutes. New track record.

October 5, 1952
Charlotte, NC. 1/2-mile dirt. Sprint car event. 10-lap heat: finished 2nd. 20-lap feature: DNS.

October 12, 1952
Terre Haute, IN. Vigo County Fairgrounds. 1/2-mile dirt. Sprint car event. 10-lap heat: finished 2nd. 20-lap feature: finished 2nd.

October 18, 1952
Raleigh, NC. 1/2-mile dirt. Sprint car event. 10-lap heat: finished 1st. 20-lap feature: finished 2nd.

October 19, 1952
Mechanicsburg, PA. Williams Grove Speedway. 1/2-mile clay. Sprint car event. 10-lap heat: finished 2nd. 50-lap feature: finished 2nd.

1953

Final Standings:
Finished 2nd in Eastern AAA Sprint car standings with 564.5 points; finished 18th in Midwest AAA Sprint car standings with 86 points; finished 38th in AAA National Championship car standings with 81.6 points.

March 29, 1953
Reading, PA. Reading Fairgrounds. 1/2-mile dirt. Sprint car event. 10-lap heat: finished 1st. 30-lap feature: finished 1st.

April 19, 1953
Trenton, NJ. New Jersey State Fairgrounds. 1-mile dirt. Sprint car event. 8-mile heat: finished 2nd. 25-mile feature: finished 1st.

May 3, 1953
Mechanicsburg, PA. Williams Grove Speedway. 1/2-mile clay. Sprint car event. 10-lap heat: finished 1st. 30-lap feature: finished 3rd.

May 10, 1953
Schereville, IN. Illiana Speedway. 1/2-mile paved. 10-lap semi: finished 4th.

June 6, 1953
Morristown, NJ. 1/2-mile paved. Sprint car event. 10-lap consolation: finished 2nd. 25-lap feature: finished 3rd.

June 14, 1953
Terre Haute, IN. Vigo County Fairgrounds. 1/2-mile dirt. Sprint car event. Time trial: 25.10 seconds. 10-lap consolation: finished 2nd. 30-lap feature: finished 3rd.

June 21, 1953
Springfield, IL. 1-mile dirt. Championship car event. Time trial: 35:16 seconds. 100-mile feature: finished 10th. *Completed 98 laps.*

July 4, 1953
Altamont, NY. 1/2-mile dirt. Sprint car event. 10-lap heat: finished 1st. 20-lap feature: finished 3rd.

July 12, 1953
Mechanicsburg, PA. Williams Grove Speedway. 1/2-mile clay. Sprint car event. 10-lap heat: finished 2nd. 30-lap feature: finished 2nd.

July 26, 1953
Mechanicsburg, PA. Williams Grove Speedway. 1/2-mile clay. Championship car event. 10-lap heat: finished 2nd. 50-lap feature: finished 5th.

August 1, 1953
Harrington, DE. Kent-Sussex County Fairgrounds. 1/2-mile dirt. Sprint car event. 10-lap consolation: finished 2nd. 20-lap feature: finished 1st.

August 8, 1953
Morristown, NJ. 1/2-mile paved. Sprint car event. 10-lap heat: finished 2nd. 25-lap feature: finished 4th.

August 15, 1953
Bedford, PA. Bedford Fairgrounds. 1/2-mile dirt. Sprint car event. 10-lap heat: finished 2nd. 20-lap feature: finished 3rd.

August 22, 1953
Springfield, IL. 1-mile dirt. Time trial: 36.22 seconds. Championship car event. 100-mile feature: completed 87 laps and awarded 12th place.

August 23, 1953
Cedar Rapids, IA. 1/2-mile dirt. Sprint car event. 10-lap heat: finished 2nd.

August 27, 1953
Sioux Falls, SD. 1/2-mile dirt. Sprint car event. 10-lap consolation: finished 2nd.

August 29, 1953
St. Paul, MN. 1/2-mile paved. Sprint car event. 10-lap consolation: finished 7th.

August 30, 1953
Milwaukee, WI. 1-mile dirt. Championship car event. 200-mile feature: finished 9th.

August 31, 1953
St. Paul, MN. 1/2-mile paved. Sprint car event. 25-lap feature: finished 1st.

September 6, 1953
Flemington, NJ. Flemington Fairgrounds. 1/2-mile dirt. Sprint car event. 10-lap heat: finished 1st. 20-lap feature: finished 1st.

September 11, 1953
Rutland, VT. 1/2-mile dirt. Sprint car event. 10-lap heat: finished 1st. 20-lap feature: finished 5th.

September 12, 1953
Syracuse, NY. 1-mile dirt. Championship car event. 100-mile feature: DPO after 50 miles.

September 19, 1953
Morristown, NJ. 1/2-mile paved. Sprint car event. 10-lap heat: finished 2nd. 25-lap feature: finished 6th.

September 20, 1953
Reading, PA. Reading Fairgrounds. 1/2-mile dirt. Sprint car event. 10-lap heat: finished 3rd. 20-lap feature: finished 5th.

September 25, 1953
Springfield, MA. 1/2-mile paved. Sprint car event. 10-lap heat: finished 2nd. 20-lap feature: finished 3rd.

September 26, 1953
Allentown, PA. Allentown Fairgrounds. 1/2-mile dirt. Sprint car event. 10-lap heat: finished 2nd. 20-lap feature: finished 1st.

September 27, 1953
Mechanicsburg, PA. Williams Grove Speedway. 1/2-mile clay. Sprint car event. 10-lap heat: finished 1st. 30-lap feature: finished 1st.

October 4, 1953
Trenton, NJ. New Jersey State Fairgrounds. 1-mile dirt. Sprint car event. 8-mile consolation: finished 1st. 25-mile feature: finished 2nd.

October 11, 1953
Reading, PA. Reading Fairgrounds. 1/2-mile dirt. Sprint car event. 10-lap heat: finished 5th. 100-lap feature: DPO after 18 laps.

October 18, 1953
Mechanicsburg, PA. Williams Grove Speedway. 1/2-mile clay. Sprint car event. 10-lap consolation: DPO. 50-lap feature: DPO. *Drove a car in the feature owned by Dutch Culp.*

October 24, 1953
Raleigh, NC. 1/2-mile dirt. Sprint car event. 10-lap heat: finished 2nd. 20-lap feature: finished 2nd.

November 1, 1953
Hatfield, PA. Montgomery County Fairgrounds. 1/2-mile dirt. Sprint car event. 10-lap heat: finished 1st. 25-lap feature: finished 4th.

November 7, 1953
Shelby, NC. 1/2-mile dirt. Sprint car event. 10-lap heat: finished 1st. 20-lap feature: finished 1st.

1954

Final Standings:
Finished 2nd in Eastern AAA Sprint car standings with 359 points; finished 20th in Midwest AAA Sprint car standings with 42 points; finished 31st in AAA National Championship car standings with 140 points.

March 28, 1954
Reading, PA. Reading Fairgrounds. 1/2-mile dirt. Sprint car event. 10-lap heat: finished 2nd. 30-lap feature: DPO.

April 4, 1954
Mechanicsburg, PA. Williams Grove Speedway. 1/2-mile clay. Sprint car event. 10-lap heat: finished 2nd. 30-lap feature: DPO after 16 laps.

April 11, 1954
Flemington, NJ. Flemington Fairgrounds. 1/2-mile dirt. Sprint car event. 10-lap heat: finished 1st. 30-lap feature: finished 2nd.

April 25, 1954
Ft. Wayne, IN. 1/2-mile high-banked dirt. Sprint car event. 10-lap heat: finished 5th. 30-lap feature: DNS.

May 2, 1954
Mechanicsburg, PA. Williams Grove Speedway. 1/2-mile clay. Sprint car event. 10-lap heat: finished 1st. 30-lap feature: DPO on 1st lap.

May 31, 1954
Altamont, NY. 1/2-mile dirt. Sprint car event. 10-lap heat: finished 1st. 30-lap feature: finished 2nd.

June 12, 1954
Schererville, IN. Illiana Speedway. 1/2-mile paved. Sprint car event. Time trial: 24.17 seconds. 10-lap heat: finished 3rd. 30-lap feature: DNS.

June 19, 1954
Langhorne, PA. 1-mile dirt. Championship car event. Time trial: 34.55 seconds. DPO while taking 2nd time trial qualifying lap. 100-lap feature: DNS.

July 5, 1954
Darlington, SC. 1 1/8-mile paved. Championship car event. Qualifying speed: 127.870 miles per hour. 200-lap feature: DPO.

July 10, 1954
Hatfield, PA. Montgomery County Fairgrounds. 1/2-mile dirt. Sprint car event. 10-lap heat: finished 3rd. 25-lap feature: finished 6th.

July 25, 1954
Mechanicsburg, PA. Williams Grove Speedway. 1/2-mile clay. Championship car event. Time trial: 27.86 seconds. 10-lap consolation: finished 5th. 50-lap feature: finished 9th.

July 31, 1954
Harrington, DE. Kent-Sussex County Fairgrounds. 1/2-mile dirt. Sprint car event. 10-lap heat: finished 2nd. 20-lap feature: finished 4th.

August 14, 1954
Bedford, PA. Bedford Fairgrounds. 1/2-mile dirt. Sprint car event. Time trial: 26.12 seconds. 20-lap feature: DNS.

August 21, 1954
Springfield, IL. 1-mile dirt. Time trial: 37.08 seconds. Championship car event. 100-mile feature: DNQ.

August 22, 1954
Cedar Rapids, IA. 1/2-mile dirt. Sprint car event. 10 lap heat: finished 2nd. 25-lap feature: finished 2nd.

August 29, 1954
Mechanicsburg, PA. Williams Grove Speedway. 1/2-mile clay. Sprint car event. 10-lap heat: finished 1st. 30-lap feature: finished 3rd.

September 4, 1954
Essex Junction, VT. 1/2-mile dirt. Sprint car event. 10-lap heat: finished 2nd. 20-lap feature: finished 3rd.

September 9, 1954
Flemington, NJ. Flemington Fairgrounds. 1/2-mile dirt. Sprint car event. 10-lap heat: finished 3rd. 20-lap feature: finished 3rd.

September 6, 1954
Flemington, NJ. Flemington Fairgrounds. 1/2-mile. Sprint car event. 10-lap heat: finished 3rd.

September 10, 1954
Rutland, VT. 1/2-mile dirt. Sprint car event. 10-lap heat: finished 3rd. 20-lap feature: finished 3rd.

September 11, 1954
Syracuse, NY. 1-mile dirt. Championship car event. Time trial: 38.62 seconds. 100-mile feature: DNP.

September 18, 1954
Indianapolis, IN. Indiana State Fairgrounds. 1-mile dirt. Championship car event. Time trial: 40.27 seconds. 100-mile feature: finished 7th.

September 23, 1954
Springfield, MA. 1/2-mile dirt. Sprint car event. 10-lap heat: finished 1st. 20-lap feature: finished 5th.

September 24, 1954
Allentown, PA. Allentown Fairgrounds. 1/2-mile dirt. Sprint car event. 10-lap consolation: finished 1st. 20-lap feature: finished 5th.

September 26, 1954
Mechanicsburg, PA. Williams Grove Speedway. 1/2-mile clay. Sprint car event. 10-lap heat: finished 6th. 10-lap consolation: finished 6th.

October 1, 1954
Reading, PA. Reading Fairgrounds. 1/2-mile dirt. Sprint car event. 10-lap heat: finished 2nd. 20-lap feature: finished 3rd.

October 3, 1954
Trenton, NJ. New Jersey State Fairgrounds. 1-mile dirt. Sprint car event. 8-mile heat: finished 1st. 15-mile feature: finished 2nd.

October 10, 1954
Reading, PA. Reading Fairgrounds. 1/2-mile dirt. Sprint car event. 10-lap heat: finished 5th. 100-lap feature: finished 9th. *Completed 94 laps.*

October 17, 1954
Mechanicsburg, PA. Williams Grove Speedway. 1/2-mile clay. Sprint car event. 10-lap heat: finished 1st. 50-lap feature: finished 7th.

October 31, 1954
Langhorne, PA. 1-mile dirt. Sprint car event. 10-mile heat: finished 1st. 25-mile feature: finished 3rd.

November 7, 1954
Phoenix, AZ. 1-mile dirt. Championship car event. Time trial: 39.17 seconds. 100-mile feature: DNP.

November 14, 1954
Las Vegas, NV. 1-mile dirt. Championship car event. Time trial: 37.98 seconds. 100-mile feature: finished 6th.

1955

Final Standings:
Finished 1st in Eastern AAA Sprint car standings with 540 points; finished 17th in Midwest AAA Sprint car standings with 66 points; finished 33rd in National Championship car standings with 100 points.

March 20, 1955
Langhorne, PA. 1-mile dirt. Sprint car event. DNQ.

April 3, 1955
Reading, PA. Reading Fairgrounds. 1/2-mile dirt. Sprint car event. Time trial: 24.60 seconds. 10-lap heat: finished 2nd. 30-lap feature: finished 1st.

April 23, 1955
Hatfield, PA. Montgomery County Fairgrounds. 1/2-mile dirt. Sprint car event. 10-lap heat: finished 2nd. 20-lap feature: finished 5th.

May 1, 1955
Langhorne, PA. 1-mile dirt. Sprint car event. 10-mile heat: finished 3rd. 30-mile feature: finished 7th.

May 8, 1955
Mechanicsburg, PA. Williams Grove Speedway. 1/2-mile clay. Sprint car event. 10-lap heat: finished 1st. 30-lap feature: finished 1st.

June 29, 1955
Langhorne, PA. 1-mile dirt. Championship car event. Time trial: 33.24 seconds. 100-mile feature: DNP.

July 10, 1955
Oklahoma City, OK. 1/2-mile dirt. Sprint car event. 10-lap heat: finished 3rd. 30-lap feature: finished 5th.

July 15, 1955
Kansas City, MO. 1/2-mile oiled dirt. Sprint car event. 10-lap heat: finished 1st. 30-lap feature: finished 10th.

July 17, 1955
Reading, PA. Reading Fairgrounds. 1/2-mile dirt. Sprint car event. 100-lap feature: finished 2nd.

July 30, 1955
Harrington, DE. Kent-Sussex County Fairgrounds. 1/2-mile dirt. Sprint car event. 10-lap heat: finished 1st. 20-lap feature: finished 1st.

July 31, 1955
Mechanicsburg, PA. Williams Grove Speedway. 1/2-mile clay. Championship car event. Time trial: 27.47 seconds. 50-lap feature: DNQ.

August 14, 1955
Carnegie, PA. Heidelberg Speedway. 1/2-mile dirt. Sprint car event. 10-lap heat: finished 3rd. 50-lap feature: finished 7th.

August 20, 1955
Springfield, IL. 1-mile dirt. Championship car event. Time trial: 37.59 seconds. 100-mile feature: finished 6th.

August 21, 1955
Cedar Rapids, IA. 1/2-mile dirt. Sprint car event. 10-lap heat: finished 2nd. 25-lap feature: finished 3rd.

August 28, 1955
Mechanicsburg, PA. Williams Grove Speedway. 1/2-mile clay. Sprint car event. 10-lap heat: finished 2nd. 30-lap feature: finished 1st.

September 3, 1955
Essex Junction, VT. 1/2-mile dirt. Sprint car event. 10-lap heat: finished 1st. 20-lap feature: finished 1st.

September 4, 1955
Flemington, NJ. Flemington Fairgrounds. 1/2-mile dirt. Sprint car event. 10-lap heat: finished 1st. 20-lap feature: finished 1st.

September 5, 1955
DuQuoin, IL. 1-mile dirt. Championship car event. Time trial: 38.48 seconds. 100-mile feature: DNQ.

September 11, 1955
Langhorne, PA. 1-mile dirt. Sprint car event. Twin 50-lap features. Time trial: 34.45 seconds. 1st 50-mile feature: finished 10th. 2nd 50-mile feature: finished 8th.

September 18, 1955
Reading, PA. Reading Fairgrounds. 1/2-mile dirt. Sprint car event. 10-lap heat: finished 2nd. 20-lap feature: finished 1st.

September 24, 1955
Springfield, MA. 1/2-mile paved. Sprint car event. 10-lap consolation: finished 2nd.

October 1, 1955
Allentown, PA. Allentown Fairgrounds. 1/2-mile dirt. Sprint car event. 10-lap heat: finished 1st. 20-lap feature: finished 1st.

October 2, 1955
Trenton, NJ. New Jersey State Fairgrounds. 1-mile dirt. Sprint car event. 8-mile heat: finished 2nd. 20-mile feature: DPO after 16 laps.

October 9, 1955
Reading, PA. Reading Fairgrounds. 1/2-mile dirt. Sprint car event. 10-lap heat: finished 2nd. 50-lap feature: finished 2nd.

October 16, 1955
Mechanicsburg, PA. Williams Grove Speedway. 1/2-mile clay. Sprint car event. 10-lap heat: finished 1st. 50-lap feature: finished 2nd.

1956

Final Standings:
Finished 1st in Eastern USAC Sprint car standings with 404 points; finished 14th in Midwest USAC Sprint car standings with 78 points.

April 18, 1956
Birmingham, AL. 1/2-mile dirt. Sprint car event. Time trial: 24.53 seconds. 10-lap heat: finished 3rd. 30-lap feature: DPO on second lap. *Hit fence.*

April 22, 1956
Mechanicsburg, PA. Williams Grove Speedway. 1/2-mile clay. Sprint car event. 10-lap heat: finished 1st. 30-lap feature: *Rained out.*

April 29, 1956
Reading, PA. Reading Fairgrounds. 1/2-mile dirt. Sprint car event. 10-lap heat: finished 2nd. 25-lap feature: finished 1st.

May 13, 1956
Atlanta, GA. Lakewood Park. 1-mile dirt. Sprint car event. 8-mile heat: finished 1st. 25-mile feature: finished 3rd.

June 10, 1956
Reading, PA. Reading Fairgrounds. 1/2-mile dirt. Sprint car event. 100-lap feature: finished 1st.

June 17, 1956
Mechanicsburg, PA. Williams Grove Speedway. 1/2-mile clay. Sprint car event. Twin 30-lap features. 10-lap heat: finished 2nd. 1st 30-lap feature: finished 3rd. 2nd 30-lap feature: finished 8th.

July 7, 1956
Allentown, PA. Allentown Fairgrounds. 1/2-mile dirt. Sprint car event. 10-lap heat: finished 1st. 30-lap feature: finished 1st.

July 22, 1956
Mechanicsburg, PA. Williams Grove Speedway. 1/2-mile clay. Championship car event. Time trial: 26.84 seconds. 10-lap heat: finished 2nd. 50-lap feature: finished 4th.

July 29, 1956
Carnegie, PA. Heidelberg Speedway. 1/2-mile dirt. Sprint car event. Time trial: 22.15 seconds. 10-lap heat: finished 3rd. 50-lap feature: finished 7th.

August 12, 1956
Mechanicsburg, PA. Williams Grove Speedway. 1/2-mile clay. Sprint car event. 10-lap heat: finished 2nd. 30-lap feature: finished 4th.

September 2, 1956
Duquoin, IL. 1-mile dirt. Sprint car event. 10-mile heat: finished 2nd. 25-mile feature: finished 5th.

September 8, 1956
Syracuse, NY. New York State Fairgrounds. 1-mile dirt. Championship car event. Time trial: 38.74 seconds. 100-mile feature: DNQ.

September 15, 1956
Indianapolis, IN. Indiana State Fairgrounds. 1-mile dirt. Championship car event. 100-mile feature: DPO after 18 miles.

September 22, 1956
Allentown, PA. Allentown Fairgrounds. 1/2-mile dirt. Sprint car event. 10-lap heat: finished 1st. 20-lap feature: finished 1st.

September 23, 1956
Reading, PA. Reading Fairgrounds. 1/2-mile dirt. Sprint car event. 10-lap heat: finished 1st. 20-lap feature: finished 1st.

September 30, 1956
Trenton, NJ. New Jersey State Fairgrounds. 1-mile dirt. Sprint car event. 8-mile heat: finished 1st. 20-mile feature: finished 2nd.

October 14, 1956
Reading, PA. Reading Fairgrounds. 1/2-mile dirt. Sprint car event. 40-lap feature: finished 2nd.

October 21, 1956
Mechanicsburg, PA. Williams Grove Speedway. 1/2-mile clay. Sprint car event. 10-lap heat: finished 2nd. 50-lap feature: finished 4th.

November 12, 1956
Phoenix, AZ. 1-mile dirt. Championship car event. Time trial: 37.70 seconds. 100-mile feature: DPO after 44 miles.

1957

Final Standings:
Finished 4th in Eastern USAC Sprint car standings with 202.5 points; finished 32nd in Midwest USAC Sprint car standings with 4 points.

March 31, 1957
Reading, PA. Reading Fairgrounds. 1/2-mile dirt. Sprint car event. 10-lap heat: finished 1st. 30-lap feature: DPO.

April 7, 1957
Mechanicsburg, PA. Williams Grove Speedway. 1/2-mile clay. Sprint car event. 10-lap heat: finished 1st. 30-lap feature: finished 2nd.

April 14, 1957
Atlanta, GA. Lakewood Park. 1-mile dirt. Sprint car event. 8-mile heat: finished 1st. 20-mile feature: DPO. *Spun out on 19th lap.*

June 16, 1957
Reading, PA. Reading Fairgrounds. 1/2-mile dirt. Sprint car event. 100-lap feature: finished 3rd.

September 15, 1957
Reading, PA. Reading Fairgrounds. 1/2-mile dirt. Sprint car event.
10-lap heat: finished 3rd. 20-lap feature: finished 3rd.

September 21, 1957
Allentown, PA. Allentown Fairgrounds. 1/2-mile dirt. Sprint car
event. 10-lap heat: finished 1st. 20-lap feature: finished 5th.

October 13, 1957
Reading, PA. Reading Fairgrounds. 1/2-mile dirt. Sprint car event.
10-lap heat: finished 1st. 40-lap feature: finished 1st.

October 20, 1957
Mechanicsburg, PA. Williams Grove Speedway. 1/2-mile clay. Sprint
car event. 10-lap heat: finished 3rd. 50-lap feature: finished 2nd.

1958

Final Standings:
**Finished 6th in Eastern USAC Sprint car standings with 97.25
points; finished 9th in Midwest USAC Sprint car standings with
78 points.**

April 13, 1958
Mechanicsburg, PA. Williams Grove Speedway. 1/2-mile clay. Sprint
car event. 10-lap heat: finished 2nd. 30-lap feature: finished 2nd.

April 20, 1958
Reading, PA. Reading Fairgrounds. 1/2-mile dirt. Sprint car event.
10-lap heat: finished 1st. 30-lap feature: finished 2nd.

June 1, 1958
Putnam, CT. Thompson Speedway. 1/2-mile paved. Sprint car event.
10-lap heat: finished 1st. 25-lap feature: finished 10th.

June 22, 1958
Terre Haute, IN. Vigo County Fairgrounds. 1/2-mile dirt. Sprint car event. 10-lap heat: finished 1st. 30-lap feature: finished 2nd.

June 29, 1958
New Bremen, OH. 1/2-mile clay. Sprint car event. 10-lap heat: finished 4th. 30-lap feature: finished 2nd.

July 27, 1958
Mechanicsburg, PA. Williams Grove Speedway. 1/2-mile clay. Sprint car event. 10-lap heat: finished 1st. 30-lap feature: DNF. *Accident with Bill Brown on lap 22.*

August 17, 1958
Terre Haute, IN. Vigo County Fairgrounds. 1/2-mile dirt. Sprint car event. 10-lap heat: finished 2nd. 30-lap feature: finished 1st.

September 7, 1958
New Bremen, OH. 1/2-mile clay. Sprint car event. 10-lap heat: finished 1st.

September 14, 1958
Reading, PA. Reading Fairgrounds. 1/2-mile dirt. Sprint car event. 10-lap heat: finished 4th. 20-lap feature: finished 7th.

September 20, 1958
Allentown, PA. Allentown Fairgrounds. 1/2-mile dirt. Sprint car event. 10-lap-heat: finished 2nd. 20-lap feature: DPO after 4 laps.

October 12, 1958
Reading, PA. Reading Fairgrounds. 1/2-mile dirt. Sprint car event. 10-lap heat: finished 3rd. 50-lap feature: DPO after 40 laps.

October 19, 1958
Mechanicsburg, PA. Williams Grove Speedway. 1/2-mile clay. Sprint car event. 10-lap heat: finished 3rd. 50-lap feature: finished 3rd.

1959

Final Standings:
Finished 1st in Eastern USAC Sprint car standings with 152 points; finished 7th in Midwest USAC Sprint car standings with 108.5 points.

March 22, 1959
Birmingham, AL. 1/2-mile dirt. Sprint car event. 10-lap heat: finished 3rd. 30-lap feature: finished 10th.

April 5, 1959
Reading, PA. Reading Fairgrounds. 1/2-mile dirt. Sprint car event. 10-lap heat: finished 2nd. 30-lap feature: finished 6th.

June 13, 1959
Mechanicsburg, PA. Williams Grove Speedway. 1/2-mile clay. Sprint car event. 10-lap heat: finished 3rd. 30-lap feature: finished 5th.

June 19, 1959
Grand Rapids, MI. 1/2-mile paved. Sprint car event. 10-lap consolation: finished 4th. 30-lap feature: DNF. *Accident on 1st lap with Bobby Grim, Leon Clum, Jim McWithy, and A.J. Foyt.*

June 21, 1959
Terre Haute, IN. Vigo County Fairgrounds. 1/2-mile dirt. Sprint car event. 10-lap heat: finished 3rd. 30-lap feature: finished 3rd.

June 28, 1959
New Bremen, OH. 1/2-mile clay. Sprint car event. 10-lap heat: finished 2nd. 30-lap feature: finished 7th.

August 16, 1959
Terre Haute, IN. Vigo County Fairgrounds. 1/2-mile dirt. Sprint car event. 10-lap heat: finished 1st. 30-lap feature: finished 2nd. *Race was flagged at 18 laps due to rain.*

September 6, 1959
New Bremen, OH. 1/2-mile clay. Sprint car event. 10-lap heat: finished 1st. 50-lap feature: finished 1st.

September 13, 1959
Mechanicsburg, PA. Williams Grove Speedway. 1/2-mile clay. Sprint car event. 10-lap heat: finished 1st. 30-lap feature: finished 1st.

September 20, 1959
Reading, PA. Reading Fairgrounds. 1/2-mile dirt. Sprint car event. 10-lap consolation: finished 1st. 25-lap feature: finished 2nd.

September 26, 1959
Allentown, PA. Allentown Fairgrounds. 1/2-mile dirt. Sprint car event. 10-lap heat: finished 1st. 25-lap feature: finished 1st.

October 11, 1959
Mechanicsburg, PA. Williams Grove Speedway. 1/2-mile clay. Sprint car event. 10 lap-heat: finished 1st. 50-lap feature: finished 1st.

1960

Final Standings:
Finished 15th in Eastern USAC Sprint car standings with 25 points; finished 17th in Midwest USAC Sprint car standings with 17 points.

April 17, 1960
Reading, PA. Reading Fairgrounds. 1/2-mile dirt. Sprint car event. 10-lap heat: finished 1st. 30-lap feature: DPO.

June 12, 1960
Terre Haute, IN. Vigo County Fairgrounds. 1/2-mile dirt. Sprint car event. Time trial: 25.56 seconds. 10-lap consolation: finished 1st. 30-lap feature: finished 4th.

July 24, 1960
Carnegie, PA. Heidelberg Speedway. 1/2-mile paved. Sprint car event. 10-lap heat: finished 4th. 10-lap consolation: finished 2nd. 30-lap feature: finished 5th.

August 7, 1960
New Bremen, OH. 1/2-mile clay. Sprint car event. 10-lap heat: finished 1st. 30-lap feature: finished 9th.

August 21, 1960
Terre Haute, IN. Vigo County Fairgrounds. 1/2-mile dirt. Sprint car event. 10-lap heat: finished 3rd. 30-lap feature: finished 11th.

September 9, 1960
Lancaster, NY. 1/2-mile paved. Sprint car event. 10-lap heat: finished 1st. 30-lap feature: finished 6th.

September 24, 1960
Allentown, PA. Allentown Fairgrounds. 1/2-mile dirt. Sprint car event. 10-lap heat: finished 2nd. 25-lap feature: finished 9th.